D1708686

ESSAYS ON DEVIANCE AND MARGINALITY

Jerry S. Maneker
California State University, Chico

University Press of America™

for Eileen, Sara, and Julie

CONTENTS

INTRODUCTION

Perhaps one of the major reasons the study of deviant behavior and marginality is a relatively popular course in the college or university curriculum is because it conjures up in one's mind such synonyms as "decay," "sleaziness," "lust" and "pervision." [1] In recent years, thanks to such scholars as Liazos [1], Quinney [2] and others [3] more taken-for-granted activities have profitably been labelled as deviant, and criminal behavior as well as law enforcement, pornography as well as censorship, indolence as well as work has been considered under its rubric.

My attempt in this volume is to first present a brief overview of major sociological perspectives in the study of deviant behavior to which many of the following chapters may profitably be related. Subsequently, I will both polemically and analytically examine what I consider to be some crucial issues and sociologically interesting phenomena related to marginality and to so-called "deviant behavior." The issue of institutionalized marginality of most of the citizenry will be dealt with in Chapter Two; the educational breeding grounds of such marginality among scholars many of whom have the somewhat ironic task of studying marginality will be dealt with in Chapter Three; work as the activity to which we devote most of our waking hours and its contribution to countering marginality as alienation from the aesthetic and moral aspects of the internal and external environment will be dealt with in Chapter Four; madness as both a possible cause of and antidote to marginality as it internally emanates and is externally imposed, as well as its rationale, will be the subject of Chapter Five. The modification of inner space through drug use and its ecstatic potential to counter both marginality and the ennui accompanying an increasingly fragmented society will be the subject of Chapter Six. The subject of one group of marginal people, elderly volunteers, and the conditions in which favorable reactions toward their work is maximum is the subject of Chapter Seven. To attempt to relate marginality to specific types of groups as points of reference, a higher level of abstraction is discussed in Chapter Eight, where a traditional sociological attempt to classify groups is hopefully furthered.

The concept of marginality is a thread that may be seen to run through this book; my attempt has been to utilize a critical perspective in studying some basic and not so basic sociological questions related to various dimensions of marginality. Some of the data and conclusions dealt with, particularly those contained in Chapter Four, are not easily empirically verifiable. Yet, I believe the study of sociology has room not only for those who may empirically codify their data, but for those of us who also delight in glimpsing chimera in their many beautiful but contradictory colors and shapes.

NOTES

1   Alexander Liazos, "The Poverty of the Sociology of Deviance: Nuts, Sluts, and Preverts," <u>Social Problems</u>, 20, 1972, pp. 103-111.

2   For example, see Richard Quinney, <u>Criminology: Analysis and Critique of Crime in America</u>, Boston/Toronto: Little, Brown and Company, 1975.

3   For example, see Clayton A. Hartjen, <u>Crime and Criminalization</u>, New York/Washington: Praeger Publishers, 1975.

Chapter One

MAJOR SOCIOLOGICAL PERSPECTIVES IN THE

STUDY OF DEVIANT BEHAVIOR

Many of us in Sociology have come to realize that "deviance" is in the eyes of the beholder. Everyone may be considered deviant depending upon the eyes from which his or her behavior is being viewed. Moreover, "marginality" is frequently both a cause and consequence of "deviance," and therefore each may usually be considered an indicator of the other. The study of deviant behavior and marginality deals with the behavior of all people as well as the stereotypes, typifications, and rationalizations that they possess and frequently impose upon other people in the creation of outsiders. The study of deviant behavior consequently deals with interpersonal (social psychological) and structural (institutional) aspects of society. The following perspectives in the study of deviant behavior to be dealt with in this chapter will therefore deal with the structural considerations as contained in the dialectical materialism of Karl Marx and the bureaucratic concerns of Max Weber and Robert Merton, as well as the other structural perspectives of Social Disorganization, Culture Conflict, Functionalism, Anomie Theory, and Labelling Theory, and Critical Theory. Differential Association and techniques of Neutralization, Near Group Theory, and Drift Theory may be seen to be major perspectives dealing more with the social psychological under-pinnings of the genesis of deviant behavior.

Karl Marx--Dialectical Materialism and its Application to Deviant Behavior.

Major ideas:
A. Class Struggle--Bourgeoisie versus Proletariat
B. Dialectical Materialism--Thesis, Antithesis, Synthesis
C. Existence and Consciousness
D. Alienation
E. Surplus Value--Labor Theory of Value; Fetishism of Commodities
F. False Consciousness
G. Imperialism
H. Substructure and Superstructure

I. Feudalism → Capitalism → Socialism → Communism

J. Communism: "From each according to his ability, to each according to his needs."

Marx[1] believed that throughout history there has been a constant struggle between the haves and the have-nots, between the rich and the poor, and the propertied and the propertyless. The two great classes that are now struggling are the bourgeoisie (the owners of the means of production: the factories and corporations) and the proletariat (people who do not own the means of production but who have to sell their labor power at the sufferance of the bourgeoisie in order to survive.)

The struggle is in the form of a dialectic in the realm of the material aspects of life, "Praxis" as Marx called it. Whereas Hegel saw the dialectic of thesis, antithesis, synthesis in the realm of ideas, Marx saw the dialectic in the material realm. Therefore, according to Marx, Feudalism (the thesis) had within it certain capitalistic elements within it (the antithesis) and this dialectic formed the synthesis of capitalism as we now know it (the synthesis). Now, capitalism is the thesis and it has within its own gravediggers, the antithetical elements of socialism, which will form a new sysnthesis of socialism where there will be a dictatorship of the proletariat and where private property will be wrested away from the Bourgeoisie. Socialism will be the transition stage between capitalism, a necessary stage in the dialectic due to its ability to provide the necessary abundance of goods and services needed for there to be a true socialism (of which there is none in the world today), and communism, the hallmark of which is "From each according to his ability, to each according to his needs."

That capitalism has within it its own gravediggers, the seeds of its own destruction, may be seen in a number of ways. Workers, given the nature of much of their work, work in association with one another and therefore can develop a community or "we-feeling" antagonistic to the bourgeoisie. Moreover, the worker is both alienated from his work and the final product of his work, given the realities of assembly line technology and inflation, as well as the rather monotonous nature of most work in capitalist society. What is also significant here is that

2

the bourgeoisie not only own the means of production and hence define the conditions of work, but also define reality for the proletariat through control of the media and the proletariat's dependence upon the bourgeoisie for survival. The ruling class has the ruling ideas and are able to impose these ideas upon others and therefore literally define reality for other people. Our discussion of "Madness at Work" in Chapter Five may be seen to be illustrative of this phenomenon.

The Labor Theory of Value shows that a product is sold for a price dependent upon its profit value rather than upon its use value, so that the profit that a company makes is primarily due to the labor that went into the product, rather than the materials of which the product is made. This profit represents the product's surplus value, of which the workers gets a minimum wage that the bourgeoisie chooses to give, and the bourgeoisie is able to take that profit and invest and reinvest it to suit its own material needs and comforts. To the degree that money yields power, power may be seen in the area of the material and in the area of the ideological. Power in the material realm may perhaps be seen most dramatically in the case of "imperialism." One of the reasons Marx felt that capitalism had within it the seeds of its own destruction was due to the fact that in order to survive, it had to increasingly expand its markets. This would eventually entail intervention in other countries for the exploitation of markets for its products. Capitalism could not stand still. Its inexorable growth would take on a life of its own in its increasingly desperate need to find markets for the products it was increasingly producing. Should potential new markets in other countries be thwarted due to a country's reluctance to have us intervene, the military might be used to facilitate our intervention, with the appropriate rationalization provided by the political and diplomatic arm of the state, which is nothing but an executive committee of the bourgeoisie, according to Marx.

Power also exists in the ideological realm as well. The ruling class has the ruling ideas. Therefore, such concepts as "deviance," and "insanity" may be seen to be both created by the material conditions in capitalistic society, and utilized as labels by the bourgeoisie and its agents to increase productivity and quash rebellion of the proletariat.

Seen in this light, it is no accident that levels of psychosis and mental hospitalization are disproportionately found among the lower classes. Drug addiction and alcoholism may be seen to be rational attempts to cope with the brutality inherent in capitalist society. Chapter Six, "Drug Use: The Institutionalization of Ecstasy" seeks to elaborate this phenomenon. Existence determines consciousness: the substructure (economic organization: means of production and relations of production) determines the superstructure (the art, ideas, religions, politics) of a society. The invidious and pejorative labels placed upon certain aspects of consciousness and superstructure may also be seen to be primarily in the possession of the ruling class.

Marx felt that when the proletariat felt any commonality of interest with the bourgeoisie, the former was suffering from "false consciousness." This false consciousness would be dispelled due to the obviousness of the internal contradictions of capitalism. Marx did not deal with the fact that rage and hostility, whether internalized or externalized, could be labelled "sick" or "criminal" (and, hence, falsely conscious) by the ruling class to protect itself against people who were too sensitive not to see through the charade. Critical Theory, to be discussed below, elaborates this phenomenon. Moreover, Marx being the humanist that he was, failed to see that when he advocated "From each according to his ability, to each according to his needs," he failed to specify who would determine what our abilities were, and who would determine what our needs were. It seems clear, given bureaucratic entrenchment, that bureaucrats would be making these decisions and judgments. The specification of the bureaucratic ethic as primarily elaborated by Max Weber and Robert Merton gives us no reason to be sanguine about how these decisions will be reached, and how these judgments will be made.

Max Weber and Robert Merton--Bureaucratic Entrenchment and its Dysfunctional Consequences

What are the major or modal characteristics of bureaucracy and bureaucrats that may give one pause in embracing Marx's vision of the future? How may these characteristics contribute to the creation and treatment of those people who have been labelled "deviant"?

4

In his treatment of bureaucracy, Max Weber,[2] a distinguished scholar, whose wide-ranging interests and studies make him a classical and valuable scholar in the sociological tradition, felt it to be the most rational and efficient method of coordinating complex tasks. To the degree that technology becomes more sophisticated, and that increasing numbers of people are needed to produce goods and services, the bureaucratic form of organization was indispensable, and of its indispensability, a definite threat to liberalism and democratic values. Weber detailed three types of "authority" in history. (Authority is distinguished from power in that the latter is the ability to coerce someone to do what you want him to do whereas the former is legitimate power, that is, power that is viewed as legitimate by both the person giving the command and by the person receiving the command. Therefore, an authority relationship exists when there is a moral compulsion to obey the command that is given.) Traditional authority is authority based upon tradition. For example, the Queen of England has authority due to the fact that her family has had authority for a long time. She does not necessarily possess any characteristics that would entitle her to the mantle of this authority other than her family membership. Charismatic authority is the second type of authority Weber delineated. In this case, authority is based upon such personal qualities of the individual as heroism, the responsibility for miracles, revelation, and so forth. Such people as Jesus, Gandhi, Moses, Hitler, Malcolm X, Martin Luther King, and Joan of Arc may be seen to have possessed authority by virtue of such personal qualities. The third type of authority that Weber delineated is Rational-Legal authority, which may be seen to form the basis of bureaucracy. Here, authority is based upon occupancy of an office or position. For example, in the military, one salutes the uniform, not the person. Respect is paid to the position one occupies and therefore obedience to a command is expected because of the office one holds. Here, authority is circumscribed, in that there are certain commands that are not considered to be legitimate, in that they do not fall within the purview of the office one occupies. For example, a professor has the right to require the student to take an exam on the subject matter of a course, but does not have the authority to order the student to shine his or her shoes. Because of rational legal authority, what power exists in bureaucracy is called "institutional power" or power that exists by virtue of one's place in an organization, and for no other reason; if one is removed from that organization, he or she no longer possesses authority or institutional power.

Other characteristics of bureaucracy that Weber elaborated in his ideal type of conception of bureaucracy were: hierarchy, division of labor, salary, career, tenure, the office is separate from the person, the person does not own the equipment he or she uses, et cetera. The rationality of bureaucracy may be seen to yield efficiency of operation and predictability of consequence and personal relationships. It is qualities such as these that Weber felt made bureaucracy very functional in our complex, modern society. It was also these qualities that led Weber to have serious misgivings about the effects upon society of the tenacity of an entrenched bureaucracy. One of the consequences of bureaucracy is that it finds work for itself in order to stay in operation. Although Weber did not deal with this specific issue, one way that a bureaucracy such as a social control agency may stay in business and increasingly perpetuate itself and generate more funds for its operation is to expand its definitions of who is deviant and falls within its purview for treatment by itself or by corollary agencies. The thesis of Chapter Five, "Madness at Work" is illustrative of this point. In this vein, elaboration of bureaucratic conditions maximizing favorable performance and attitudes toward one's work in the absence of financial remuneration is the subject matter of Chapter Seven, "Motivation and Structure in Volunteer Work." The issue here is that given the nature of bureaucracy and the characteristics of its incumbents as elaborated by Merton, people are coerced into doing things that they might not otherwise do, and impose bureaucratic values upon other people and situations that may be both inappropriate and destructive of themselves and others.

Robert Merton[3] showed how the very functions of bureaucracy could be seen to yield dysfunctional consequences. Given the rationality of bureaucracy, its structure has direct effects upon the personalities of the people who work within it. The rationality and predictability of bureaucracy yields incum-

bents who are "methodical, prudent, disciplined."
Adherence to the rules becomes an end in itself and
therefore the original goal for which the bureaucracy
was developed becomes displaced. The means (rule
adherence) therefore frequently become ends in themselves. This ritualism works both to the detriment
of clients of the bureaucracy, the workers in the
bureaucracy, and the effectiveness of the bureaucracy
itself. An example of some of the destructive effects
of such ritualism is seen in Chapter Three, "Some
Consequences of Educational Socialization," and in
Chapter Four, "Work and Political Conservatism: A
Sexual Thrust."

It has been suggested by Robert Michels that
bureaucracy yields a renunciation of far-reaching
outlooks.[4] Bureaucratic structure has definite
effects upon the ideas of people. However, as
distinct from the view of Karl Marx, ideas may also
be seen to be generators of action and structure.
Max Weber posited in his book, The Protestant Ethic
and the Spirit of Capitalism,[5] that religious ideas,
such as those contained in the Protestant ethic (for
example, that work is noble and a glorification of
God; that people could lend money at interest) could
be the cause of or a necessary factor in the development of an economic system (in this case, capitalism).
In this vein, we may speculate about a bureaucratic
mentality and its effects upon people, their relationships, and upon bureaucracies and society itself, as
Chapters Two through Seven seek to do.

Social Disorganization

Such terms as "social disorganization" and
"social pathology" were synonyms for "deviance" in
the 1930s through the 1950s. They have come into
disuse for the same reason that "deviance" should
come into disuse. They are pejorative concepts that
have a decidedly middle class bias, and by empha-
sizing "negative" phenomena, omit the study of many
behaviors that could also be profitably studied under
its rubric. For example, the brutalities we engage
in everyday and have normalized could profitably be
studied under its rubric, but usually are not. Moreover, what appears to be "disorganized' from an outsiders' point of view usually may be seen to have a
definite organization, meaningful to the participants
in the social system. In his classic study of a slum

and its alleged disorganization, William F. Whyte in
Street Corner Society[6], for example, masterfully
sketched its structure and meaning to its inhabitants.

It is perhaps for reasons such as these that the
term "social disorganization" is no longer in vogue.
Yet its value bias and perspective, particularly in
the types of behaviors conventionally classified as
"deviant" by both laymen and most sociologists, are
still very much with us. The Chicago School[7] was
undoubtedly the well-intentioned forerunner of this
perspective. They empirically demonstrated that
delinquency rates were substantially correlated with
slum conditions and that as one moved out of the inner
city the rates progressively declined. This perspective disputed notions of biological or psychological
inferiority as causes of various types of deviant
behavior, and attributed such behavior to such
negative conditions as squalor, poverty, population
congestion, and broken homes. The burden for deviant
behavior was not only removed from the back of the
individual and placed in the nature of the social
structure, but the causative agents of such behavior
were seen to be remediable.

That social structure effects one's behavior
can hardly be argued. Moreover (and therefore perhaps
because) this belief is the cornerstone and funda-
mental justification for the discipline of sociology.
However, the social disorganization perspective does
not account for such phenomena as people in the slums
who do not become criminals, and for people in middle
class areas in homes where the mother and father are
both present who do become criminals. "Differential
Association," to be discussed below, attempts to
address this phenomenon. This lapse is not to fault
the perspective of social disorganization, since no
one perspective or theory can account for all the
myriad and complex variables associated with a given
social phenomenon. However, it seems that this
perspective does not adequately do justice to many
of the current questions in the area of deviant behavior being asked and the proffered explanations.
"Critical Theory," to be discussed below, seeks to
deal with some of these questions and explanations.

Culture Conflict

When we talk of "culture" we are talking of the
norms, values, beliefs, and artifacts of a group of

people. A culture binds a people together and does a great deal to help insure continuity from one generation to another. Moreover, culture is made possible by language and by comparing languages we can see that certain terms that correspond to a way of looking at the world that characterizes or is a part of one culture cannot adequately be translated into the language of another culture that looks at the world differently. A given culture, therefore, specifies world views, proper and improper behavior, rituals, deities, and rationalizations in order to make sense out of the world and in order to assure some predictability of behavior. All people are socialized into at least one culture, and behave and think according to the precepts of that culture. What is considered "normal" is therefore culturally determined and, hence, culturally relative. Similarly, what is considered "deviant" is also dependent upon the values of the cultural agent making the definition. What is considered "normal" in one culture may be considered "deviant" in another culture, just as what is considered "deviant" at one time may be considered "normal" at another time in history.

There is no one culture in our country. Indeed, our country is made up of a number of subcultures, each with its own values, beliefs, and even language that is distinct but may overlap with other subcultures or with the dominant culture, which may be labelled as White, Middle-Class and Protestant. Although this dominant culture has such values as deferment of gratification, neatness, upward mobility, academic intelligence, and verbal fluency, these values are by no means shared by some of the subcultures in our society. There are ethnic subcultures, occupational subcultures and social class subcultures. Subcultures may come into conflict with one another or a subculture may come into conflict with the dominant culture, or through immigration, for example, one culture may come into conflict with another culture.

Some of the consequences that occur when cultures collide was admirably detailed by William I. Thomas and Florian Znaniecki in <u>The Polish Peasant in Europe and America</u>,[8] which is a classic work in sociology. Two major theories related to subcultures and juvenile delinquency that have been most compelling in sociology are those propounded by Albert Cohen and Walter Miller. Albert Cohen[9] accounts for lower class gang delinquency by stating that lower-class boys accept middle-class values but due to deprivation cannot compete effectively with middle-class boys. Therefore, they engage in "reaction formation" (a Freudian concept) and seek to show their contempt for the middle-class values they actually respect by engaging in non-utilitarian delinquent behavior. Walter Miller[10], on the other hand, sees lower class delinquency as representing values that are in the tradition of the lower-class itself and as a natural emanation of the lower class. Such values, or as he calls them "focal concerns," are toughness, smartness, trouble, excitement, fate, and autonomy. From this perspective, Cohen's view may be seen as a middle-class view that sees lower-class delinquency as a reaction to the middle class due to envy. Miller sees the conflict due to a difference in values between the lower class itself and the dominant middle class. To my knowledge, data that exists cannot preclude taking both views seriously at this time. Given this stage of our knowledge, however, it seems safe to posit that agents of the dominant culture who have the power and influence through political, military, economic, and media control to define what is normal and what is deviant according to their values, will codify those values both into "commonly accepted" rules of deportment as well as into the law itself.

Differential Association and Techniques of Neutralization.

The attempt to address the question we asked above concerning how we may account for the fact that one person brought up under "unfavorable" conditions (such as in the slums) becomes a criminal while another person brought up under ostensibly similar conditions does not become a criminal is the major thrust of Differential Association theory.[11] In essence, this theory states that criminal behavior is learned; the same principles of learning take place as occur in the learning of any other kind of behavior. Whether one becomes a criminal or a professor, certain techniques of the role and certain attitudes, expectations, and behavior associated with the given role are learned. The basic elements

of Differential Association theory are as follows:
(1) Criminal behavior is learned; (2) It is learned
in the process of interaction with persons in a
process of communication (both verbal and the communication of gestures); (3) The principle part of the
learning of criminal behavior occurs within intimate
personal groups. (According to Edwin Sutherland, who
formulated this theory, the media play a relatively
unimportant part in the genesis of criminal behavior.
However, that is a matter of opinion, data that
exists to the best of my knowledge can neither support
nor refute this contention.); (4) When criminal behavior is learned, the learning includes: (a) techniques of the crimes, and (b) the appropriate motives,
drives, rationalizations, and attitudes; (5) The
specific direction of motives and drives is learned
from definitions of the legal codes as favorable or
unfavorable. (A culture conflict may be seen to
exist here since some definitions are favorable and
others are not favorable.) The core of the theory
is as follows: (6) "A person becomes delinquent because of an excess of definitions favorable to
violation of law over definitions unfavorable to
violation of law." When a person becomes criminal,
he/she does so because of an overabundance (in terms
of frequency and/or duration and/or priority and/or
intensity) of contacts with criminal patterns and
also because of relative isolation from anti-
criminal patterns. As Daniel Glaser pointed out
"From the standpoint of Sutherland's theory, any
correlate of crime must be shown to effect an individual's learning experience if it is to be thought
of as having a causative function in his criminality
..." Moreover, in utilizing Sutherland's theory,
we should pay attention to all reference groups of the
individual (groups with which he/she identifies), and
not just his/her membership groups (groups of which
he/she is a member) in tracing the social influences
of an individual's behavior.[12]

As mentioned in Differential Association theory,
not only appropriate behaviors and techniques are
learned in taking on the role of "criminal," but the
appropriate rationalizations for that role. Gresham
Sykes and David Matza[13] elaborated upon five such
rationalizations to which juvenile delinquents frequently resort. The authors feel that since most
delinquent youth have some acceptance of conventional
values, they must neutralize their conventional ties
and moral scruples before they can commit delinquency.

11

Hence, their term for those rationalizations:
Techniques of Neutralization. These techniques of
neutralization comprise the following: (1) the denial
of responsibility (for example, attributing their
behavior to slum conditions or bad parents); (2)
denial of injury to the victum; (3) the denial of
the victum (for example, justifying attacks on
homosexuals due to the latter's status); (4) the
condemnation of the condemners; (5) the appeal to
higher loyalties (for example, the loyalties of
friendship may be a rationalization used by a person
breaking the law). We all have attitudes and rationalizations concerning what we do based upon our experiences, associations, and the problems we face.
Delinquents and criminals are in this way no different
from us.

Near Group Theory and Drift Theory

Although in my opinion, Near Group theory is
not a particularly compelling one, it is useful in
demonstrating how a self-fulfilling prophecy may
work in creating the very thing we ostensibly fear.
Lewis Yablonsky[14], who developed this theory, says
that delinquent gangs can neither be categorized as
a group (characterized by such factors as a defined
leadership, network of roles and communication,
meaningful interaction between and among the members)
nor as a mob (the polar opposite of a group, being
based upon the emotions of the moment and no defined
leadership, permanence or network of roles). A
delinquent gang may be seen to fall mid-way on a
continuum between group and mob. A near-group will
eventually disband and not normally shift to group
status or mob status if left alone. However, such
groups as newspapers, criminologists, social workers,
and police, by treating the near group as a group,
insisting upon organization and leadership, can
create a self-fulfilling prophecy whereby this
originally false definition of the situation becomes
true by virtue of this treatment and the near group
does in fact become a group.

Drift Theory as propounded by David Matza[15] is
congruent with Near Group Theory in that it supports
the notion that most people drift in and out of
deviance. Most delinquents if left alone may be
expected to drift out of delinquency the more
approaching manhood eliminates masculinity and status

anxiety. We may see that by labelling them as
delinquent and treating them as delinquent, we may do
alot to confer a criminal status upon them permanently
both oficially and as it effects their concept of
self. To the best of my knowledge, insufficient data
exists to either support or refute this contention.
Such labelling may reinforce delinquent or deviant
behavior; it may provide for rationalizations for
that behavior; or, particularly if the person is
not especially committed to that behavior (as in
most cases of shoplifting, for example), may extin-
guish that behavior in the future.[16]

Anomie Theory

The term "anomie," first used as a sociological
concept by Emile Durkheim,[17] means normlessness,
powerlessness, the state whereby one's aspirations
or expectations exceed what the social structure can
deliver. Durkheim's study of suicide incorporated
"anomie" in one of the types of suicide. He felt
that suicide rates, being more constant than even
death rates cross culturally, could be attributed not
to psychological, biological or geographic factors,
but to social facts. He saw these social facts as
(1) degree of integration of the group to which one
belonged, and (2) amount of regulation the group
exercised over the individual. The first social
fact contained two types of suicide: (1) Egoistic
Suicide, where suicide occurs because one is not
sufficiently integrated into his/her group; (2)
Altruistic Suicide, where suicide occurs because one
is too much integrated into his/her group. (Examples
of altruistic suicide are usually found in the
military, such as Kamikaze pilots, or one who
throws his body on a grenade to protect other people
in his squad.) The second social fact contains two
types of suicide: (1) Anomic Suicide, where suicide
occurs because of normlessness, as in an economic
or political crisis in a society (such as an economic
depression); (2) Fatalistic Suicide, where suicide
occurs because the norms of a society or group are
too oppressive, and the individual may be seen to be
driven to suicide.

Robert Merton[18] elaborated Durkheim's notion
of "anomie" and defined it as a dysjunction between
the cultural goals of a society and the legitimate
(or institutionalized) means available to people to
achieve those desired goals. Legitimate means are

13

not equally accessible to everyone to achieve cultural
goals we have been socialized to desire. This in-
equity is defined as "anomie". Merton posits five
possible modes of adaptation to anomie, the last four
of which may be defined as deviant behavior: (1) Conformity, where the individual adheres to the cultural
goals and the legitimate means to achieve them; (2)
Innovation, where the individual adheres to the
cultural goals, but does not adhere to the legitimate
means to attain them (for example, a bank robber
adheres to the cultural goal of acquiring wealth, but
does not adhere to the legitimate means of acquiring
it); (3) Ritualism, where the individual does not
care about the cultural goals, but does adhere to the
legitimate means to achieve the goals (this example
of ritualism may be noted in the goal displacement
that may be seen to occur in some social service
agencies, where the goal of helping people is sub-
ordinated over time to the adherence to rules, which
may on occasion militate against realizing the
original goal); (4) Retreatism, where the individual
rejects both the cultural goals and the legitimate
means to achieve them (for example, chronic alcohol-
ics and the adaptive activities of psychotics); (5)
Rebellion, where the individual rejects both the
cultural goals and the legitimate means to achieve
them and substitutes his/her own goals and means.
"Rebellion" was later classified by Merton as "non-
conforming behavior," whereas innovation, ritualism,
and retreatism are classified as "aberrant behavior."[19]
In our discussion of Critical Theory, such deficits
this theory shares with most others such as value
bias and assumed homogeneity of values, as well as
acceptance of the prevailing political definitions
of reality will be discussed. Moreover, as access to
"legitimate means" to achieve desired cultural goals
increases such chances of attainment, Cloward and
Ohlin[20] point out that access to "illegitimate means"
may also serve the same purpose. For example, lower-
class boys may find access to jobs in the numbers
racket with far greater ease and facility than do
middle-class boys.

<u>Functionalism</u>

Functional theory as elaborated by Talcott
Parsons[21] is at a high level of abstraction. To try
to make this theory more concrete, I see it as
composed to two major approaches. The first one,
begun by Emile Durkheim[22] and excellently elaborated

by use of historical data by Kai Erikson[23], sees deviant behavior as a necessary component in society. Deviant behavior adds to the stability of society by giving us groups of outsiders to identify against so as to increase our own self esteem, by helping to define the boundaries or outer limits of acceptable behavior in the society, by creating and cementing in-group cohesion by creating an "us" versus "them" situation. Deviant behavior is therefore viewed as functional for the stability and integration of a society, and it is socially created for that reason. Increased rates of deviance can therefore be seen in times of crises of identity of societies. For example, Erikson demonstrates that witches arose in New England at a time when they were needed to help come to grips with the failure of the great experiment of the Puritans to live by God's law on earth. The witches, and Quakers before them, were not only scapegoats but also an outgroup against which the ingroup could identify and hence reinforce their beliefs and prejudices as well as try to solidfy an increasingly tenuous in-group cohesion.

Beyond these considerations, this approach of the functional perspective indicates that deviant behavior is very profitable for agents and agencies of social control. Such people as law enforcement personnel, corrections officers, judges, lawyers, social workers and criminologists are employed because of deviant behavior; it is to their interests to increasingly expand the scope of their activities in order to further increase their job security and develop increasing hegemony over their respective domains. Therefore, given these considerations, the last thing social control agents and agencies want is to eradicate deviance. Quite the opposite is more likely the case.

In addition, deviant behavior is functional for the participants. It is an axiom that people continue to engage in behavior that is rewarding for them or is more rewarding than perceived and/or actual alternatives, despite what such outsiders as law enforcement personnel or middle-class criminologists may view as rewarding. Both Kingsley Davis[24] and Ned Polsky[25] have elaborated this point in analyses of prostitution and pornography respectively. Davis indicated how prostitution, far from being a threat to the institution of the family was very functional in contributing to its stability by being a stigmatized safety valve mechanism providing for transitory, not necessarily socially acceptable sexual behavior and acts. Davis showed that to the degree that sexual behavior was confined to the marital bond and to only some specified acts, such a safety valve mechanism as prostitution was necessary for the stability of the family and of society. Polsky used the same reasoning in discussing the functional utility of pornography. Whereas prostitution provides for the expression of non-familial, antisocial, transitory sex with a person, pornography does so via fantasy. Pornography exists in every literate culture and is functional in that it serves as an aid to masturbation. In this connection, Polsky reminds us of a definition of a pornographic book as a book that one reads with one hand.[26]

The second approach in the name of Functional Theory largely deals with the work of Talcott Parsons, a leading exponent of functional analysis, whose work, though still influential, reached its zenith in the late 1950s. I find it easiest to conceptualize his contribution to the study of deviant behavior by discussing his notions of "reciprocity of expectations" and "pattern variables." The functional view sees the parts (roles) of the social system as being interrelated; if a change is made in one part, it effects other parts in some way. When two people interact in a social system they do so in reference to certain cultural norms. Meaningful interaction is therefore not only possible in a society, but also quite predictable. People with different interests can, by understanding and tacitly agreeing to abide by the cultural norms defined as appropriate to the given situation, interact quite successfully and predictably. This phenomenon is called a "reciprocity of expectations" where one person's (Ego) expectations of the other's (Alter) behavior act as sanctions upon alter to behave in the way ego expects and alter's expectations of ego's behavior act as sanctions upon ego to behave in the way alter expects. It is this reciprocity of expectations that makes meaningful interaction and therefore society possible. Both socialization of children and adults helps insure that they internalize the cultural norms of the given society and behave in reference to them. To the degree that socialization is incomplete or inadequate, agents of social control help insure that interaction occurs in reference to these norms. Although deviance can be functional for a society by serving as an impetus for change, it does disturb the equilibrium of that society and beyond a certain point cannot be tolerated. When the reciprocity of expectations does not occur, deviance exists. Clearly the emphasis of this school upon equilibrium and its desirability, as well as their non-reflective acceptance of the legal and middle-class political definitions of reality, omits such questions from consideration as the benefits of deviance to a society, the possible benefits of restructuring our society with increasing humanitarian concerns, and the personal and social costs of our labelling and treatment of so-called deviants in our society.

The frustration or non-reciprocity of one's expectations that can be labelled as "deviant" when two people interact also has a collective dimension where the normative expectations of a group or society may not be adhered to by a person or group of people. Such non-adherence may be seen upon examination of "pattern variables." Pattern variables, according to Parsons, may be both utilized as a tool for the analysis of interaction by the sociologist and as a series of dilemmas that are resolved by an individual upon interacting in a given situation. It is in their latter capacity that we shall discuss them. The choices that an individual makes based upon his definition of the situation are as follows: (1) Affectivity (being emotional in the situation) versus Affective Neutrality (neutralizing one's emotions in the situation); (2) Ascription (responding to who a person is) versus Achievement (responding to what a person has achieved); (3) Self orientation (trying to maximize one's own gains in the interaction) versus Collectivity orientation (being primarily interested in the welfare of the group); (4) Universalism (applying the same standards to each person in the situation) versus Particularism (applying different standards to different people in the situation); (5) Specificity (relating to only one aspect of the other person) versus Diffuseness (relating to the other as a whole person). Clearly, the nature of the choices one makes will be dependent upon his/her definition of the situation, and his/her definition may either be erroneous or inappropriate as the choice or choices he/she makes in resolving these dilemmas of interaction may not meet the expectations of others in that situation and/or be congruent with the cultural norms defined as appropriate to that situation. For example, we expect a teacher to resolve the dilemmas of interaction in the following way: (1) Affective Neutrality, to be "professional"; (2) Achievement oriented, to respond to what a person has achieved in class rather than upon such consideration as the wealth of the student's family; (3) Collectivity orientation, to be more concerned with the intellectual well being of the class rather than his/her own profits; (4) Universalism, to use the same basis of evaluation for all his/her students and to not show favoritism; (5) Specificity, to relate to the individual's intellectual needs rather than to such needs as emotional or sexual needs. Of course, these choices are not exclusive in that elements of both horns of each dilemma are utilized. The issue here is predominance of choice. Given our normative expectations of a teacher's behavior in the classroom, the teacher who exhibits the above patterns of behavior is considered to be conforming to the normative expectations of our society in regard to his/her role. However, should he/she exhibit a culturally inappropriate choice or series of choices, his/her behavior would be considered "deviant" and increased socialization would be attempted (such as the principal talking with him/her) or social control would be manifested (such as firing him/her).

People may only have a limited commitment to a system of relations or may over-commit themselves to a system of relations. Each of these modes of orientation, considered deviant and potentially threatening to the equilibrium and stability of the social system, may be seen to have both an "active" and a "passive" form. The active form of alienation may be expressed as aggressiveness and/or incorrigibility; the passive form of alienation may be expressed as withdrawal (as in mental illness) and/or evasion. The active form of overconformity (empirically impossible to measure) may be expressed as dominance and/or compulsive enforcement (such as ritualism, discussed above). The passive form of overconformity may be expressed as submission and/or perfectionism (which may also be seen to be ritualistic). Parsons views these as alternative forms of deviant behavior.

18

This aspect of functionalism appears to reify deviance and emphasize its negative aspects as it relates to possible disequiliburim of society. More importantly, it accepts current conventional definitions of deviance and neither views these definitions as arbitrary nor as having hardly more justification than to protect the status quo and the material interests of the people in power in the given society. The attempt to remedy these deficiencies occur in the next two perspectives: Labelling Theory and Critical Theory.

Labelling Theory

Labelling or Interactionist Theory is humanistic, if nothing else. Whereas biological, psychological, psychiatric and most sociological theories see the individual as the initiator of one's deviance, to some degree aided and abetted by the social structure, Labelling Theory places the burden upon the reactions of "conventional people" in the social structure. Howard S. Becker[27] was the first to cogently formulate this perspective. He said: "...<u>social groups create deviance by making rules whose infraction constitute deviance</u>, and by applying those rules to particular people and labelling them as outsiders... From this point of view, deviance is <u>not</u> a quality of the act a person commits, but rather a consequence of the application by others of rules and sanctions to an 'offender.' The deviant is one to whom that label has successfully been applied; deviant behavior is behavior that people so label."[28]

Therefore, this perspective states that meaning is imputed to behavior; meaning is not inherent in behavior or events. Deviance, like all social life, is a social construction of people in a given society. Hence, what is considered deviant from one point of view may not be considered deviant from another point of view; what is considered as deviant varies in time and space. For example, making pornographic films may be considered deviant in the United States in the twentieth century but not necessarily considered as deviant in Sweden in the twentieth century or perhaps in the United States in the twenty-first century. Another example regarding different points of view as to what is "deviant" might see middle-class people viewing chronic welfare recipients as deviant, while some of the latter could view many of the former who work most of their waking hours at jobs they can barely tolerate as "deviant."

What is considered as deviant is therefore a matter of point of view and since the politically dominant portion of the population (not necessarily representing the majority, as can be seen in South Africa as of the time of this writing) largely determines social, economic and political reality, they also define what is deviant and support social control agencies in containing, treating, or disposing of people who are offensive or threatening to them. As we create meaning in our lives and impose meaning upon situations and events, we also create deviants. This labelling perspective says that it is in our defining of deviance and deviants that they are socially constructed and not otherwise inherently "deviant." For example, as Chapter Five, "Madness at Work" suggests, the labelling of behavior as "normal" or as "eccentric" or as "mental illness" is largely a product of the perspective and world view of powerful people in a society and has enormous ramifications for the further status and "treatment" of the individual.

There are several criticisms that can and have been made of this perspective. Jack Gibbs[29] has perhaps specified the most cogent of them by stating that labelling theory is not a theory but a perspective (which could probably be said of all the theories dealt with here), and is more a theory of reactions to deviance than a theory about deviance itself. Moreover, how severe does a reaction have to be before the behavior is recognized as deviant; "(W)hy do some persons commit the act while others do not?" "(W)hy is the act in question considered deviant and/or criminal in some societies but not in others?"[30] To date, it does not seem that these criticisms have been adequately or sufficiently addressed.

Critical Theory

Critical Theory is a logical and political extension of Labelling Theory. More frequently than not it embraces the Marxist perspective in seeing criminal law and the creation of outsiders as means by which the state protects Capitalism and particularly that one percent of the population that owns forty percent of the nation's wealth. This perspec-

20

tive is viewed as humanistic and its proponents seek
to provide alternative images of a possible society
where the creation of crime and deviance would not be
useful to a certain class of people as it is now. One
of the most prolific exponents of this perspective is
Richard Quinney[31], who has concentrated his work in
the area of criminology. He feels that crime is both
a matter of definition (behavior against which there
is a criminal law) and is politically motivated.
Criminal law therefore serves a dual function in
society: (1) it provides the means of registering,
signifying, degrading and stigmatizing a person as a
criminal and then (2) it provides itself with its own
justification. Law thus provides the means and the
authority to criminalize the behavior of a person.

Certain groups in a society have the power to
have their interests, invariably class-based, enacted
into law and they have the power to impose their will
upon others; the state is created by the capitalist
class to protect its own interests against people or
groups who are perceived as threats to its domain.
Traditional criminology, by accepting conventional
views of crime and criminals, has usually served as a
handmaiden to the state in seeking to control "crime"
and punish people the state defines as "criminals."
Quinney and most others embracing this perspective
feel that criminologists and sociologists rather than
serving the ruling class must provide alternative
images of a just society to people and have a class
conflict analysis of crime. Quinney feels that
crime and criminal behavior are closely tied to the
organization of society into classes. No behavior is
objectively criminal; all behaviors are "social" and
they only become criminal when they have been
offically defined as criminal by authorized agents of
the state, and any behavior could theoretically be
so defined.

Critical Theory therefore posits that the causes
of crime are not necessarily in individuals but in
the basic institutions of our society. Quinney
summarizes his views of criminal law and hence the
"problem of crime" bluntly: "(1) American society
is based on an advanced capitalist economy. (2) The
state is organized to serve the interests of the
dominant economic class, the capitalist ruling class.
(3) Criminal law is an instrument that the state and
dominant ruling class use to maintain and perpetuate
the social and economic order. (4) Crime control

in capitalist society is accomplished by institutions and agencies established and administered by a governmental elite, representing dominant ruling class interests, to establish domestic order. (5) The contradictions of advanced capitalism -- the disjunction between existence and essence -- requires that the subordinate classes remain oppressed by whatever means necessary, especially by the legal system's coercion and violence. (6) Only with the collapse of capitalist society, based on socialist principles, will there be a solution to the crime problem."[32]

As with all perspectives, Critical Theory has certain shortcomings. First of all, I believe it must explore dimensions beyond the confines of a Marxist or Neo-Marxist analysis of society. There are many types of crime that would resist these confines without torturing logic--for example, the crime of rape (Eldridge Cleaver's ambivalent justification[33] before further incarceration and being "born again" notwithstanding) or of child molesting. Moreover, Critical Theory does not deal with the issue of why some poor people commit "crimes" while others do not, or why crimes exist in ostensibly more socialist societies. In addition, even if capitalism were eradicated, such domination based upon bureaucratic elitism or some other basis of stratification could yield definitions of certain behaviors as being criminal to protect the new ruling class. If the aim of the proponents of this perspective is to eradicate stratification, they have provided no blueprint or even a hint of how this eradication might take place or of how we could be reasonably certain that non-stratification would be viewed as desirable or workable, or that stratification based upon other criteria would not arise to fill the vacuum. These criticisms of Critical Theory are not meant to deprecate its value, since I feel far more affinity with it than I do with any of the other perspectives discussed. However, if Critical Theory is to realize its promise and live up to its potential, I feel that these issues will have to be addressed.

Although the critical perspective, more broadly defined, can perhaps be seen in most of the chapters of this book, its imposition upon the social structure and the ubiquitousness of marginality is perhaps most fully drawn in Chapter Two, "The Institutionalization of Marginality."

NOTES

1. Karl Marx, "Manifesto of the Communist Party," in Robert C. Tucker, ed., The Marx-Engles Reader, New York: W. W. Norton and Company, Inc., 1972, pp. 331-362; Friedrich Engels, "On the Division of Labor in Production," in Robert C. Tucker, op. cit., pp. 321-327; Karl Marx, "Capital: Selections," in Robert C. Tucker, op. cit., pp. 191-317.

2. H. H. Gerth and C. Wright Mills, From Max Weber: Essays in Sociology, New York: Oxford University Press, 1972, pp. 196-264.

3. Robert Merton, "Bureaucratic Structure and Personality," In Robert Merton, Social Theory and Social Structure, New York: The Free Press, 1968, pp. 249-260.

4. Robert Michels, "Assimilation of the Discounted into the State Bureaucracy," in Robert Merton, et al., Reader in Bureaucracy, New York: The Free Press, 1952, p. 142.

5. Max Weber, The Protestant Ethic and the Spirit of Capitalism, translated by Talcott Parsons, New York: Charles Scribner's, 1958.

6. William Foote Whyte, Street Corner Society: The Social Structure of an Italian Slum, Chicago: University of Chicago Press, 1943.

7. See for example, R. E. Park, E. W. Burgess, and R. C. McKenzie, The City, Chicago: The University of Chicago Press, 1925; Clifford R. Shaw, The Natural History of a Delinquent Career, Chicago: University of Chicago Press, 1931; Clifford R. Shaw, The Jack Roller: A Delinquent Boy's Own Story, Chicago: The University of Chicago Press, 1930.

8. William I. Thomas and Florian Znaniecki, The Polish Peasant in Eurpoe and America, Chicago: University of Chicago Press, 1918.

9. Albert Cohen, Delinquent Boys: The Culture of the Gang, New York: The Free Press, 1971, pp. 49-72; 121-137.

10. Walter Miller, "Lower Class Culture as a Generating Milieu of Gang Delinquency," in David O. Arnold, ed., <u>The Sociology of Subcultures,</u> Berkeley: The Glendessary Press, 1970, pp. 54-63.

11. Edwin Sutherland and Donald R. Cressey, <u>Criminology</u>, Philadelphia/New York/Toronto: J. B. Lippincott Company, pp. 75-77.

12. Daniel Glaser, "Role Models and Differential Association," in Earl Rubington and Martin S. Weinberg, eds., <u>Deviance: The Interactionist Perspective</u>, New York: The Macmillan Company, 1972, pp. 326-330.

13. Gresham Sykes and David Matza, "Techniques of Neutralization: A Theory of Delinquency," <u>American Sociological Review</u>, 22, December, 1957, pp. 667-670.

14. Lewis Yablonsky, "The Delinquent Gang as a Near Group," <u>Social Problems</u>, 7, Fall, 1959, pp. 108-117.

15. David Matza, <u>Delinquency and Drift</u>, New York: John Wiley and Sons, Inc., 1964, pp. 1-32.

16. Daniel Glaser, <u>Social Deviance,</u> Chicago: Markham Publishing Company, 1971, pp. 41-50.

17. Emile Durkheim, <u>Suicide: A Study in Sociology,</u> translated by John A. Spaulding and George Simpson, New York: The Free Press, 1966, pp. 241-276.

18. Robert Merton, "Social Structure and Anomie", in Robert Merton, <u>Social Theory and Social Structure</u>, op cit., pp. 185-214.

19. Robert K. Merton, "Social Problems and Sociological Theory," in Robert K. Merton and Robert A. Nisbet, <u>Contemporary Social Problems: An Introduction to the Sociology of Deviant Behavior and Social Disorganization,</u> New York: Harcourt, Brace and World, 1965, pp. 723-24.

20. Richard A. Cloward and Lloyd E. Ohlin, <u>Delinquency and Opportunity: A Theory of Delinquent Gangs,</u> New York: The Free Press of Glencoe, 1964, pp. 144-160.

21. Talcott Parsons, <u>The Social System,</u> Glencoe:
    The Free Press, 1951.

22. Emile Durkheim, <u>The Division of Labor in Society,</u>
    translated by George Simpson, Glencoe: The
    Free Press, 1960, p. 102.

23. Kai Erikson, <u>Wayward Puritans: The Study in the
    Sociology of Deviance</u>, New York: John Wiley and
    Sons, Inc., 1966.

24. Kingsley Davis, "Prostitution," in Robert Merton
    and Robert Nisbet, ed., <u>Contemporary Social
    Problems,</u> New York: Harcourt, Brace and World,
    1961, pp. 262-88.

25. Ned Polsky, <u>Hustlers, Beats and Others,</u> Garden
    City: Doubleday and Company, Inc., pp. 183-200.

26. <u>Ibid.</u>, p. 187.

27. Howard S. Becker, <u>Outsiders,</u> New York: The Free
    Press of Glencoe, 1963.

28. <u>Ibid.</u>, p. 9.

29. Jack P. Gibbs, "Conceptions of Deviant Behavior:
    The Old and the New," <u>Pacific Sociological</u>
    Review, 9, Spring, 1966, pp. 9-14.

30. <u>Ibid.</u>, p. 12.

31. See for example, Richard Quinney, <u>Criminology:
    Analysis and Critque of Crime in America,</u>
    Boston/Toronto: Little Brown and Company, 1975,
    Richard Quinney, <u>Critique of Legal Order: Crime
    Control in Capitalist Society,</u> Boston, Little
    Brown and Company, 1974.

32. Richard Quinney, Criminology, <u>op. cit.,</u> p. 291.

33. Eldridge Cleaver, <u>Soul on Ice</u>, New York: McGraw-
    Hill, 1968, p. 14; p. 18.

Chapter Two

THE INSTITUTIONALIZATION OF MARGINALITY

"Action Sociology" may be seen to come to analytical and empirical terms with Mills' dictum that we must view history and biography as an interrelated whole.[1] Only when people become conscious of their community of interests, and develop a "sociological imagination," can they be inclined to relieve themselves of guilt attendant upon accepting the burden for their alienation or anomie and place that burden where it frequently belongs: on the social structure. There are two interrelated approaches one takes in the area of action sociology, therefore. The first approach, as witnessed in this chapter, is to awaken consciousness--or dissipate "false consciousness."[2] This can be done by sociologically analyzing common human and social problems and by making people aware of these analyses so that a community of recognized interests may be awakened. The second approach occurs in the "field", where the sociologist, on the basis of the first approach, mobilizes motivation to redress grievances and help organize strategy to satisfy that motivation.

Marginality seems to be one of the most pervasive and yet little known institutions in our society. Until we analytically and empirically come to grips with this realization, action sociology and the attendant mobilized motivations remains an ideal rather than a viable alternative to apathy and alienation.

To postulate that marginality is institutionalized in our society implies three concurrent phenomena. The first phenomenon relates to the definition of "institution." An institution is an established way of doing things.[3] It is usually functional for the society of which it is a more or less viable locus. The pervasiveness of marginality, to be discussed below, seems to be a well established principle to infer that it is similarly established in our society. The second phenomenon relates to the definition of "marginality."[4] This term may be seen to be the structural correlate of the social psychological conditions of alienation and anomie. Here, the individual is in a social structural twilight zone within a more or less acceptable institutional frame-

work. He/she is on the outside looking in, and frequently sees distorted images, projected by his/her
perceptions of the reality. The third phenomenon
suggests the functional utility of marginality (in
line with the first phenomenon). We each have a
vested interest (to be discussed below) in keeping
ourselves and each other marginal. It seems functional for society as a whole (not a reification, but
with a contemporary Durkheimian[5]perspective) that
many individuals and subgroups become and remain
marginal to other individuals, subgroups, and
dominant organizations and other institutions in
society.

The preceding discussion sets the stage to
analyze who is marginal and why. Here we are not
interested in types of marginal people, but in the
pervasiveness of marginality, its apparent genesis,
and its raison d'etre (or its functions).

Who is marginal? Children,[6] adolescents,[7]
women,[8] minority groups, "deviants,"[9] people on
welfare, the poor,[10] and the aged.[11] Most people,
either at some time in their lives or throughout all
their lives, are marginal. But marginal to what?
They seem to be marginal to the social patterns that
are expected on the basis of their socialization.
That is to say, most people are marginal to a reference group they have been socialized to regard
highly. For children and adolescents it is adulthood.
For Negroes, it is white people. For the poor, it is
the middle class. For "deviants," it is acceptance,
or benign neglect by "straights." For the aged, it
is acceptance by young and middle-aged representatives
of the youth culture.[12] In these and in many other
cases, people are marginal to a more or less highly
valued reference group. One may argue that if one
is an integrated member of a subculture, such as that
of drug addicts, there is not any outside reference
group that he/she regards highly. This may be true
were the subculture contained in a vacuum. However,
the potential power of the outgroup to harass and
punish the members of this subculture of definition
forces members of that subculture to act with no
little regard to that outgroup--or, here, reference
group, given their behavior in psychological and
social reference to that "dominant group." Cohen [13]
lends credence to this assumption in his study of
delinquency. His view is that juvenile delinquency is
a form of natural adaptation to the working class

environment. The working class youth is exposed to middle class values which he cannot attain because of social structural constraints. He resolves his dilemma by contriving with others who share in his plight to adjust. They do this by inverting middle class values and denigrating them. Thus arises the delinquent subculture. The details of Cohen's theory are specified in Chapter One. Here, we are interested in its suggestive implications for social structural contingencies fostering marginality. The working class youth ostensibly has a reference group, the middle class. Yet, he is barred from effective participation with members of that class. Hence, his marginality. To deal with that marginality more or less effectively, he transforms that reference group into an outgroup which both facilitates the formation of an ingroup and allows him some vehicle for retribution on members of the middle class and their values.

Of course, this does not mean that all people who act in reference to other people are marginal. It does mean that when people use certain others to develop an identity of self, and act in regard to those others, be they in proximity to them or not, they view that identification group as a reference group. If they want to make that reference group a membership group and have not as yet been able to do so, they may be viewed as marginal with reference to that group. Although marginality may, and frequently does, occur in reference to one's membership group, we are only interested here in the type of marginality broadly conceived as the social structural correlate of alienation (being estranged from existing norms) and anomie (the absence of norms).

Viewed in this way, we may ask why are so many people marginal? There appears to be two major reasons why so many people are marginal. It will be the discussion of these two reasons that may shed light on one's community of interests with others that may help awaken consciousness of the role of the social structure in the genesis of the functionally useful control mechanisms of marginality. The two reasons deal with the following two concepts: "identity" and "frontiers."

Identity is that which gives one a sense of self. It is dependent upon the way we are socialized and who does the socializing.[14] The former element denotes the "content" of the socialization; the latter element denotes the "form" of the socialization. McLuhan's premise that the form of communication effects the individual far more than does its content,[15] leads us to emphasize the latter element in our discussion of identity. Who does the socializing? In other words, given that the content of socialization acts as a control mechanism internalized by the individual (some call it a "superego"), what role does the form of the socialization--that is, who does the socializing and under what conditions-- have in identity development? We should also emphasize that socialization does not stop at any particular age, but goes on throughout one's life. Indeed, we feel that "adult socialization" may even be of greater importance in identity development than is socialization that occurs in one's childhood. Since socialization is learning gotten via communication, and since the form of communication does not necessarily have to take second place to its content, it seems fruitful to examine the role of "form" in identity development.

For our purposes, there seem to be two major kinds of identity: "primary identity" and "secondary identity." These terms denote from what groups (and, hence, relationships) one derives his concept of self. We are a mobile people.[16] Given the requirements of the nuclear family and job, occupational and geographical mobility are unbiquitous phenomena in our society.[17] Such conditions of life seem to require relationships that are secondary rather than primary in nature. A primary relationship usually occurs in a primary group characterized by intimate face to face interaction.[18] This type of relationship is characterized by diffuseness, affectivity and particularism.[19] The relationship is diffuse in that one responds to another as an integrated whole; a whole human being. In this relationship one is interested in the other person as a total human being. The relationship is affective in that one responds to another with feeling, not solely with intellect. There is emotional investment here, where the individual deeply cares what happens to the other human being. Involved here is some "transference" and "identification" where the individual is happy or sad, proud or mortified on the basis of the actions of the other in the primary relationship. The relationship is particular in that expectations of the other's behavior are held up to standards predicated upon emotional involvement with the other human being in the relationship. In short, we usually have different standards for our loved ones than we do for the local shop keeper.

A secondary relationship is characterized by specificity, affective neutrality, and universalism.[20] It usually occurs in a secondary group, which is usually large and has a formal structure. The office, the schoolroom, et cetera are apt examples. The relationship is specific in that one responds to the other as a segment--for example, as an economic person. The major interest one presumably has in his/her employee is that of a worker. He/she usually does not care how happy or fulfilled the other is, unless it has bearing on his/her performance at work. He/she does not view the other as a whole person. The relationship is affectively neutral in that the person usually does not invest his/her emotions in the being of the other. The relationship is universalistic in that the individual applies standards of expectations to the other that in no way takes the others' unique characteristics, such as they may be, into account.

Secondary relationships are not only unbiquitous in our society, but seem to be increasingly playing the role of foremost socializing agent. From the time one enters school, he/she is involved in secondary relationships with significant others (friends who when in class become other schoolmates who usually approve and disapprove behavior). These significant others are teachers and peers. Their orientation toward the person are by and large affectively neutral, specific, and universalistic. The individual not only becomes a manipulable object, but increasingly comes to view himself/herself in that light with seemingly little if any cognitive dissonance (holding two inconsistent beliefs).[21] He/she comes to learn, if he/she is to gain acceptance, he/she must please others--all sorts of others. This feeling is reinforced throughout secondary school and college. The college student quickly learns that the only sure way of doing well in a course is to memorize the instructors' notes and regurgitate them at exam time. The material need not be relevant, and frequently is not relevant; it need not be stimulating; it need not expand the horizons of the student. It need fill only one criterion: it must be memorizable. Many students appear to become anxious when asked to express their ideas. Some seem devoid of ideas in a broad subject area, and many more appear to fear the

ridicule of their fellow students should they appear
too dense or too profound.

School then may be seen to become a training
ground for the stereotyped organization man. The
person who works hard and forgets what for. The
person reluctant to question anything. Higher education has as its ideal goal to turn out scholars.
We may define a scholar as one who questions every-
thing--"everything". Not only do college graduates
seem reluctant to question anything, but have a
vested interest in not questioning anything--par-
ticularly if it pertains to the social structure.
They have a vested interest in being apathetic. Their
apathy may be seen to spring from their marginality,
and reinforce that marginality, by encouraging
blindness to effective alternatives to cope with the
contingencies of their existence. We seem to have a
vested interest in keeping ourselves apathetic, and
hence marginal. By remaining marginal, we seem
better able to set up boundaries that reaffirm our
identities.

We may be seen to have a vested interest in
keeping ourselves marginal because of the type of
identity we have developed. We need boundaries
based on apathy to reaffirm an existence and not a
life. Moreover, we have a vested interest in keeping
ourselves apathetic, lest the extent of our marginality create cognitive dissonance, with our sense of
individuality (read "rugged individualism"). The
type of identity that seems to require apathy as
both a necessary condition as well as a defense
mechanism we call "secondary identity." Its opposite
is "primary identity."

Primary identity, one formed usually in the context of primary groups and primary relationships, is
a core identity that affirms one's existence as a
human being. A view of one's sanctity as a human
being seems involved here, where one feels fulfilled
as a person, and one with his or her community. Here,
the individual does not have to justify his/her existence to himself/herself either through work or the
accumulation of wealth and other material goods.
Just his/her "being" in and of itself justifies his/
her existence in his/her own eyes. He/she regards
himself/herself affectively, particularistically, and
diffusely, since his/her socialization primarily
occurs in such a context of primary relationships.

We are concerned here with secondary identity. Here, the individual views himself/herself as a manipulable object. He/she not only feels constrained to act in regard to others, but to have a concept of self predicated upon who and how many he/she is able to please. The correlative attitude has been called "other direction."[22] This type of identity may be found in the form of an organizational chart, symbolized by the folded hands of the schoolchild who rather early in the game comes to realize that the teacher rewards discipline far more than he or she does creativity. It is found in the philosophy of the draftee that he just has to "put in" two years. It is found in the philosophy of the college student that he/she just puts in four years so that he/she can attain what he/she considers to be some measure of financial security. It is found in the philosophy of the graduate student who is willing to put up with all kinds of indignities so that he/she may become a "doctor." It is found in the philosophy of the faculty member who will keep his/her mouth shut "until I am promoted and given tenure." It is found in the philosophy of the struggling worker who loudly sings the praises of free enterprise, even if he/she cannot afford to pay for an operation for his/her spouse. Secondary identity seems unbiquitous and institutionalized in our society by both apathy and a rigid adherence to belief in our "ideal culture" (what we say exists) rather than in our "real culture" (what actually exists.)

Given the predominance of secondary relationships, identity is up for grabs. It depends upon the type of others with whom one has specific, universalistic, and affectively neutral relations. We have suggested above how identity gives us a vested interest in maintaining our own marginality. It will now be our task to suggest how identity crises, coupled with the constriction of frontiers, gives us a vested interest in maintaining the marginality of others. Marginality serves as a very effective control mechanism. What better way to avoid insults, unpleasant people, or their condition than by constructing boundaries to facilitate their "keeping their distance?" The key to the executive washroom is, therefore, more than a perquisite or accoutrement of status. It is a boundary maintaining mechanism insuring the marginality of certain others as well as one's own. More symbolically, titles, such as doctor, professor, Mr., et cetera, may not be terms

denoting respect as much as they formalize relationships to insure the marginality of the interactants,
which also reinforces one's secondary identity.

If secondary identity yields marginality, and
if marginality reinforces secondary identity, we each
have a vested interest in keeping ourselves and others
marginal to minimize dissonance with our secondary
identity which is functional to our basically mobile,
organizational, instrumental, way of life. Marginality may not only be seen as a control mechanism, but
also as a "frontier." There are very few, if any,
frontiers open to the average person in American
society today. Horatio Alger stories are quite uncommon. One does not start farming without any
capital. Most young people today do not want to own
businesses, nor do they find the odds in their
favor.[23] Where are the challenges? Where are the
frontiers that cement ingroup feeling? It appears
that one of the paradoxes of our existence is that
we have to create marginality if we are to have some
amount of ingroup feeling. This ingroup feeling is
instrumentally attained and fills utilitarian functions
consonant with the needs of our secondary identity.
If there can be said to be one law in sociology it is:
when there is a threatening outgroup, the ingroup will
unite to defend itself against that threatening outgroup.[24] Marginality seems the major vehicle by
which we develop we-group feeling. What cements
people of the middle class to each other? What helps
maintain their community of interests? It is the
creation of outgroups comprised of people who usually
have the middle class as a reference group and who are
therefore marginal. People cheating on welfare; why
don't the poor work and better themselves like we
did?; there is no end to the spiraling of taxes; why
don't these radical young punks shave, take a bath,
and go out and work for a living? Here, we have a
vested interest in creating and maintaining the marginality of others, so that we can establish some
small measure of identity beyond that of a manipulable
object, so that we can justify our existence. In the
1960's it must have been nothing short of obscene to
a man who had "worked hard" for thirty years, and
still had trouble making ends meet, to have seen so
many young people eschew that kind of life and flaunt
seemingly dissonant values in his face. To legitimate much of the past thirty years, the man frequently felt constrained to in turn eschew those dissonant
values by imputing negative qualities upon the bearers

of those values. Hence, marginality is created and
is functional not only as a control mechanism, but
also functional as a device to perpetuate middle-
class values.

We therefore appear to have a vested interest in
being marginal and maintaining the marginality of
others. One of the reasons has been stated as the
perpetuation of middle-class values. In addition to
the above perceived examples, one more may suffice
to indicate the prevalence and pervasiveness of this
phenomenon before we finally sew this crazy quilt
of patches. In most of our dealings with other people
we seem to value appearance far more than we do competence. This even is the case when competence would
seem to be sorely needed and advantageous. For example, picture a typical man applying for a job. He
makes sure he is clean shaven, his hair is cut pro-'
perly. He is wearing a conservative suit, (if he is
applying for a white collar position), and comports
himself with mannerly decorum. Should a man applying
for a job as an engineer, for example, show up for
his interview in dungarees and needing a shave, it is
highly questionable whether he would be offered the
job, regardless of his credentials, or competence.
Appearance is not only a tool of impression management, it is a major way of becoming integrated in or
alienated from a reference group. We can easily
develop a community with others depending upon how
we dress. The worker wears overalls, the doctor
wears his "whites", the Shriner wears his fez. These
are not only symbols of status, but serve to separate
the wearer from others not of that group. The
wearer alienates others and is himself alienated.
Such alienation as we have seen is functional as both
a control mechanism (to keep others at a distance);
as a way of reinforcing our secondary identity so that
we can more effectively cope in a mobile society primarily made up of secondary relationships as a means
of creating ingroups through the creation of outgroups; as a way of perpetuating middle-class values.

The analysis of marginality as an institution in
and of itself is interesting. It sheds light on a
social phenomenon that is not only significant but
quite relevant to all of us in our complex, hetero-
geneous, industrial society. But the major aim of
this discussion has been to set the stage for a dis-
course on what we have termed "action sociology," and
its role in the general area of sociology. In turn,

by discussing the role of sociology as a humanistic discipline in a liberal arts education, we may better view the role of action sociology as a contribution to that education. Marginality is one institution among others, many of which to some extent also alienate us from others, and serve to place us on the periphery of ongoing activity engaged in by members of our reference groups. To analyze marginality in this way does not in and of itself contribute to action sociology or to the relevance of the analysis to the scholar. What does give it its relevance is its use in awakening consciousness and dispelling false consciousness about one's place in society, so that meaningful alternatives one may use in coping with contingencies of his or her existence are explored to the fullest. This should not only be the role of action sociology, or of sociology itself,[26] but of a liberal arts education as well.

At the beginning of this chapter the broad outlines of action sociology were sketched to set the stage for the analysis of marginality as an institution. It will now be our task to use our analysis of marginality as a way of specifying the function of action sociology for sociology and for a liberal arts education. H. Laurence Ross states: "...A Sociological education can inform students of the nature of social constraint; of the fact that norms, values and beliefs are social in origin rather than biological or physical. It can explain the mechanisms that sustain cultural prescriptions, the relations between culture and personality that result in individuals' bearing the culture without consciousness of this fact. Sociological theory implies that what might be good or functional for the group as a whole may not necessarily be in the best interests of individual members of the group, and that individuals may resist group prescriptions and at times be better off for their resistance. It furthermore implies that deviation can be a source of desirable social change, which in the long run may result in greater utility for the majority of the group members. The awareness of social constraints, then, can be said to increase individual freedom, by suggesting that the alternatives for action in consequential situations are greater than previously imagined. ...this potential for individual freedom and rational action is the core of sociology's contribution to the liberal education."[27]

Understanding marginality, therefore, may aid us in developing a community of interests in light of the social constraints that engender and are an outgrowth of that marginality. An additional requisite for awakening consciousness seems to be that we not only view sociology as a science (if it can be said to be a science, which is an entirely different problem) but as a humanistic discipline. Marginality and its consequences seem to take on more startling propostions when viewed within a humanistic sociological framework.

Sociology may be viewed as a humanistic discipline not only for the sociologist but for the undergraduate--and in many ways primarily for the undergraduate--as well. How can it be viewed as a humanistic discipline? First of all it helps us understand the society we live in. We become acquainted with many different values and beliefs extant in that society many of which may or may not be our own. We learn about many of the institutions of that society, such as family, religious, governmental, economic, and stratification institutions. We learn about certain behaviors some of which are defined as criminal or deviant and why this is so. We also learn that people have vested interests in foisting their values upon others, and institutionalize middle class values in our criminal laws and in our definitions of what is acceptable and not acceptable (that is, deviant) in our society. We also become acquainted with many social problems in our society and explore their causes and possible solutions in the context of our social structure and its institutions. We also learn about the "mechanics" of our society, such as bureaucracy, methods engendering conformity in society, and methods of challenging the status quo.

Secondly, sociology helps us understand others. We learn about the "stuff" of interaction embodied in our mutuality or reciprocity of expectations. We learn that if interaction is to proceed relatively smoothly, we must be able to quite accurately predict other people's responses to our behavior; they must be able to quite accurately predict our responses to their behavior. We also learn about dilemmas confronting "disadvantaged" people in our society. We learn about being poor in a relatively affluent society; we learn about leisure time in a society to some extent valuing the Protestant or work ethic. We also learn about personal problems attendant upon the existing configuration of the social structure

and its institutions and values. One example is
social pressures engendering mental illness.[28]

Thirdly, sociology helps teach us "relativism"
as a guiding principle. We learn that there is
nothing intrinsic in the quality of any act that
makes it "abnormal." We learn that such a definition
is predicated upon certain values which may be influential in shaping the fate of one who exhibits
behavior offensive to that set of values. We also
learn that there is a wide range of what we call
"normal." Human behavior differs according to one's
place in history; one's ideologies, biology (sex,
size, and so on), geography, caprice, health, one's
status in the class hierarchy, education, happiness,
and these and many other qualities in others one
confronts everyday. Therefore, "deviance" can be
"normal" in another time, in another place.

Finally, sociology helps us understand ourselves.
We learn about the process of socialization, or how
we become a "self". We learn the mechanics of the
development of an identity of self. We also learn
about the impingements of our own and other people's
values upon us; the impingements of the mechanics
and institutions and other social forces upon us and
how we confront them and come to terms with them. For
example, a major question that sociology seeks to address is: "How does the individual (read "I") become
tractable to social controls?" When we come to terms
with the answers to this question, we learn that much
more about ourselves and about our place and role in
the social structure.

Action sociology is an attempt to realize the
promise of sociology as a humanistic discipline. By
making us aware of our community of interests, we take
the first step in seeking and effecting solutions to
social and personal problems the core of which lie in
the social structure. By recognizing that most of us
share a common fate of marginality, and the reasons
for this fate, derivative grievances may be redressed
by mobilizing motivation to change appropriate parts
of the social structure. It is the role of action
sociology to not only help mobilize this motivation,
but to suggest strategic points in the social
structure in which intervention may occur. Finally,
the sociologist may, on the basis of his or her
knowledge of the social structure, help people alter
the social structure to effect the changes they

desire. Here, knowledge is put to use in a very real way. We do not become social engineers, but social therapists. We are physicians and society is our patient. If certain people want to solve a problem, and the sociologist also perceives it as a problem, and feels he/she can be of help, he/she makes use of his/her knowledge in redressing the grievances.

Sociology holds out the promise of aiding us in better understanding ourselves, our society and its institutions, and our relationship to those institutions. We may not only use our knowledge in transmitting cultural values, but in altering those values. We do not only become a science, but become a profession. By articulating our expertise in the field we may help our society thrive and aid people in living lives that they feel will be most fulfilling and meaningful for them. In this way we not only pay lip service to the promise of sociology, but elevate the discipline through our service to those we study. Our promise may be realized, people may be helped, our knowledge will be applied. Involved here is a recognition that no problem is beyond solution if motivation is mobilized, and we make full use of our knowledge and courage. What better incentive to study sociology?

NOTES

1. C. Wright Mills, The Sociological Imagination, New York: Grove Press, Inc., 1961.

2. Karl Marx, and Frederick Engels, The German Ideology, New York: International Publishers, 1947, pp. 16-17.

3. Leonard Broom and Philip Selznick, Sociology: A Text with Adapted Readings, Evanston, Illinois: Row, Peterson and Company, 1960, p. 27.

4. Everett V. Stonequist, "The Marginal Man": A Study in Personality and Culture Conflict, New York: Charles C. Scribner's Sons, 1937.

5. Emile Durkheim, The Rules of Sociological Method, Chicago: University of Chicago Press, 1938.

6. Who should be "seen and not heard."

7. Edgar Z. Friedenberg, Coming of Age in America, New York: Random House, Inc., 1965.

8. Betty Friedan, The Feminine Mystique, New York: Dell Publishing Company, 1964.

9. Howard S. Becker, Outsiders: Studies in the Sociology of Deviance, New York: The Free Press, 1966.

10. Michael Harrington, The Other America; Poverty in the United States, Baltimore: Penguin Books, 1968.

11. James E. Birren, ed., Handbook of Aging and the Individual, Chicago, University of Chicago Press, 1959.

12. Talcott Parsons, Essays in Sociological Theory, New York: The Free Press of Glencoe, 1954, pp. 89-103.

13. Albert K. Cohen, Delinquent Boys: The Culture of the Gang, Glencoe: The Free Press, 1955.

14. George Herbert Mead, Mind, Self and Society: From The Standpoint of a Social Behaviorist,

41

Chicago and London: The University of Chicago
Press, 1963.

15. Marshall McLuhan and Quentin Fiore, <u>The Medium
is the Message</u>, New York: Random House, 1967.

16. Paul B. Horton and Chester L. Hunt, <u>Sociology,</u>
New York: McGraw-Hill Book Company, 1968,.p.278.

17. Eugene Litwak, "Occupational Mobility and Extended Family Cohesion," <u>ASR</u>, 25, February,
1960, pp. 9-21; "Geographic Mobility and
Extended Family Cohesion," <u>ASR</u>, 25, June,
1960, pp. 385-394.

18. Leonard Broom and Philip Selznick, <u>op. cit.,</u>
pp. 124-127.

19. Talcott Parsons and Edward A. Shils, eds.,
<u>Toward a General Theory of Action: Theoretical
Foundations for the Social Sciences,</u> New York
and Evanston: Harper and Row, Publishers,
1962, pp. 76-88.

20. <u>Ibid.</u>

21. Leon Festinger, Henry W. Riecken, and Stanley
Schacter, <u>When Prophecy Fails,</u> Minneapolis;
University of Minnesota Press, 1956.

22. David Riesman, Nathan Glazer, and Reuel Denney,
<u>The Lonely Crowd: A Study of the Changing</u>
American Character, Garden City, New York:
Doubleday Anchor Books, 1953, pp. 34-38.

23. C. Wright Mills, <u>White Collar: The American
Middle Classes,</u> New York: Oxford University
Press, 1956, 1953, pp. 63-68.

24. Muzafer Sherif, "Experiments in Group Conflict"
<u>Scientific American,</u> 195, 1956, pp. 54-58.

25. Erving Goffman, <u>The Presentation of Self in
Everyday Life,</u> Garden City: Doubleday and
Company, Inc., 1959, pp. 208-237. For a
more detailed analysis of the role of appear-
ance in analyzing impressions see Erving
Goffman, <u>Stigma; Notes on the Management of
Spoiled Identity</u> Englewood Cliff, New Jersey;
Prentice-Hall, Inc., 1964.

26. See H. Laurence Ross, "The Teaching of Sociology In the Metropolitan College," _The American Sociologist,_ 1, May, 1966, pp. 143-144.

27. _Ibid.,_ p. 143.

28. See, for example, August B. Hollingshead and Frederick Redlich, "Social Stratification and Psychiatric Disorders," _American Sociological Review,_ 18, April, 1953, pp. 153-169.

Chapter Three

<u>SOME CONSEQUENCES OF EDUCATIONAL SOCIALIZATION</u>*

> "In (the movie) <u>The Graduate</u>, as in
> upper middle-class America generally,
> parents relate to their children in a
> somewhat vampiresque way. They feed
> on the child's accomplishments, sucking
> sustenance for their pale lives from
> vicarious enjoyment of his or her de-
> velopment. In a sense, this sucking
> is appropriate since the parents give
> so much--lavish so much care, love,
> thoughtfulness, and self-sacrifice on
> their blood bank. But this is little
> comfort for the child, who at some
> point must rise above his guilt and
> live his own life--the culture demands
> it of him. And, after all, a vampire
> is a vampire." [1]

In his perceptive book, Philip Slater here calls
attention to what we may call "institutionalized
vampirism" endemic, not only in middle-class America,
but within much of civilization as a whole. Such
institutionalized vampirism may be seen in many
phases of one's life: the family, the work situation,
the economic structure, etc. However, this vampirism
may be seen most readily and, indeed, poignantly
within schools; its existence not only describes
various attendant phenomena, such as "alienation"
and "apathy" but may be seen to go a long way toward
explaining the rather harsh realities of much of the
bareness of "the intellectual life." Just as the
reality shock many people experience upon entering
academic life is profound, so is the impact of "anti-
intellectualism" with the academy. There has always
been a history of such anti-intellectualism in our
country, but only within the past decade does it
seem to have taken root within the ivory tower
stronghold that had hitherto acted as a buffer and
protection for the academic against this onslaught.

The major purpose of this paper is to seek to
explain seeming "alienation" and "apathy" among
students, the underpinnings of which may be seen to
lie a thinly veiled, and not too well disguised contempt for the academic life. (I don't believe we are

important enough as academics in the students' lives to be deserving of their hostility.) Moreover, the reality shocks many of us have upon establishing a career in academia may also be partly explained via the vehicle of institutionalized vampirism. That the existence of this vampirism within graduate school life (which will be the focus of this paper) is not obvious to all of us, may I think be in part accounted for by the "mystification of experience,"[2] that is so important to the socialization of the future academic. The basis of that socialization, and its relationship to the realities of "the intellectual life" will now be explored.

To mystify an experience is to make it into what it is not. Through the alchemy of mystification one is taught to view a negative experience as being "positive" or at least justifiable. As Laing says: "Children are not yet fools, but we shall turn them into imbeciles like ourselves, with high I.Q.'s if possible."[3] We mystify the robotization of our students and through the magic of alchemy transform our perception of it (and frequently even their perception of it) as being necessary, just and even rewarding. When the alchemy does not affect their perception, however, and when the students are not convinced that their best interests are being served by the academy and its functionaries, their "rebellion" may take the form of demonstrations, but far more frequently takes the form of compulsive docility, seeming inability to become excited by ideas or the life of the mind, seeming inability to grasp abstractions of even the simplest nature. We dislike their brutishness, for, I suggest, within that brutishness we see ourselves—and we see ourselves as we were as graduate students.

To seek to understand the underpinnings of the "institutionalized vampirism" and the "mystification of experience" that occurs in graduate school, I would like to discuss the processes, content, outcomes, and prospects of graduate school socialization. One of the most salient features of the graduate school experience seems to be its "irrationality." In professional schools such as those dealing with law, medicine, dentistry, and so forth, there may be seen to be a predictable career (or predictable sequence of steps) one goes through for a specified number of years. In these schools the student know. that in one year he will be in the shoes of the

46

person who is now one year ahead of him, should he be able to master the subjects that he is now taking. There is a sense not only of an integrated order, but also a sense of "progress as one moves from one step to the next. In graduate school on the other hand this is not usually the case. In Sociology, for example, it is viewed as a "horizontal" rather than a "vertical" discipline. In the latter case, one course presupposes knowledge of another course, as is usual in the aforementioned types of school. However, Sociology is viewed as a perspective, the acquiring of which need not be done in any particular sequence or serial order. Indeed, there does not seem to be such a regular sequence established. This being the case, not only is there little inherent order, but little sense of "progress," and hence, no predictable career.

Coupled with the lack of a predictable career is the further "irrationality" of the thesis. By irrationality in this context is meant no clear or even necessary connection between means and ends. The fostered dependence upon "advisors" who carefully examine every word, whose likes and dislikes, biases and preferences must be known and adhered to by the student is the reality of the trauma of the dissertation. Ideas do not seem to be as important as the judicious interpretation of data; the long view and the perspective on the subject does not seem to be as important as the survey of literature (the accuracy of which is hardly at issue); the love of learning is not at all relevant--or certainly not as relevant as the laborious process of revising one's way into the academic fraternity. Moreover, the word "advisor" may be seen as a euphimism. In reality he frequently becomes the unpredictable policeman who fondles his club without necessarily striking one with it--although the injunction is clear that he may, and that he has, and that he can. Academic life is filled with horror stories of graduate students thinking that they had come to the end of their graduate school career, only to have their "advisors" tell them that their questionnaire had to be reworded, new data had to be obtained, etc. This element of irrationality bespeaks not only institutionalized vampirism, but a cruelty of a most unspeakable nature.

Mystification of these experiences notwithstanding, these horror stories are not isolated
occurrences but seem to occur relatively frequently.
Their occurrence, moreover, does not stem from evil
people using dependent students to fill their ego
needs. Their occurrence is institutionalized within
the educational institution and is part and parcel
of the reality of everyday life of the student within it. Creativity is risky in these leagues; docility and conventionality are more frequently and
regularly rewarded. What creativity that is likely
to occur occurs within the narrow framework of the
advisor's prejudices and the most conventional
literature and studies done in the given field.
Moreover, the utmost in creativity is institutionally
encouraged not in reference to the subject matter,
but in reference to the playing of the role perceived as acceptable to one's "advisor." The mystification of the graduate school experience comes
full circle when the student successfully introjects
the roles and biases of his advisor and the other
"relevant" faculty who hold the club over his career
and life chances to the point where he actually comes
to see the rationality of their actions and perceptions. The near panic reaction of the carpet
being pulled from under the student who has committed
several years to a goal that can be snatched from
him with no more than a cursory acknowledgment, and
with no possibility of redress, becomes transformed
upon the awarding of the degree to a conventional-
ized narcissism, not of the intellectual or physical
self (which wouldn't be so bad) but of the "academic"
trappings that represent the most conventional values
both of the academy and of the middle-class society
in which one lives. With this stance, "form" becomes
more important than "content." This is not only true
of the thesis, but of the relationship of the student
to his advisor.

Although the form may be at least as important
as the content of the processes of socialization of
the graduate student, there are some telling aspects
of the content that seem worth exploring. Coupled
with the "irrationality" of the curriculum, it is
very rare in just my experience that the graduate
student receives less than a "B" in a course, frequently and usually independently of his performance.
Since a "B" average is required, most instructors
have an unwritten code of giving a "B" except in
unusual circumstances. Therefore, not only is the

eventual outcome of career contingencies (the awarding
or not of the degree) to a great degree independent of
content (or performance, or grade) but the grade itself is also to a great degree independent of such
performance.

The narrow, irrelevant, punishing thesis sets
the tone of the hazing ceremony that is part and
parcel of the initiation of the student into the
academic fraternity. However, the content of this
aspect of socialization suggests to the student that
a contribution to knowledge (which, through the
mystification of experience, a dissertation is
supposed to represent) and knowledge itself is similarly punishing and relatively dull. In the dissertation, the hypotheses are narrow, frequently divorced (or made to be divorced) from the real world, and
also frequently divorced from substantive theory.
(Just take a look at dissertation titles). Thus,
the relationship of data to theory, analysis to
interpretation, and the intellectual life to life
itself, appears strongly and awesomely remote. Yet,
through the mystification of the experience, we
obtain the results of this socialization--and we
obtain them with a vengence. Some of these negative
results may be enumerated as follows: (1) the
"Getting Even Syndrome." Here, the professor, perhaps
unwittingly, seeks to get back at his own students
to make them go through what he did or at least have
them appreciate what he had to go through. As
Farber[4] points out, the professor thus makes his
accomplishments seem awesomely remote from the possible grasp of the student. (2) the "Subversion of
Scholarship." For many professors, the last research
they do is the dissertation. In light of the above
discussion, one need not wonder why. (3) Within the
academic profession, there is the encouragement of
docility and "safe" people, both intellectually and
politically safe. Many examples have been related
to me of people who were refused academic appointments
because of their political involvements or because
they were engaged in research that threatened the
faculty. Again, in these examples, it was not the
content of the research that seemed to bother the
faculty, but the fact that the applicant was engaged
in research at all that seemed threatening to them.
How widespread this phenomenon, or in what elements
of academic life it usually exists, is merely a
matter of conjecture at this point. But concrete
research in this area would be most interesting, and

I suspect, compelling. (4) The encouragement of the retreat into bureaucracy--and a reliance upon that bureaucracy for upward mobility. This desire for upward mobility, so much a part of our culture is frequently antithetical to a life of scholarship-- where one follows his muse and stands by his convictions regardless of the consequences. (5) The encouragement of timidity results both in the "getting even syndrome" and the opposite syndrome which embodies the pandering after student approval. It may be seen that such things as student evaluations of faculty not only increase this timidity and make the professor more vulnerable to bureaucratic approval, but frequently encourages the already timid professor to pander after student approval, not only for ego needs (for the ego isn't too noticeable by this time), but for career and life-chance needs.

Given the nature of educational socialization, here depicted in the graduate school, the harvesting of the above results have been obtained and will be increasingly obtained in the future. Some of these prospects may be seen as follows: (1) There will be increased bureaucratic controls over the seemingly hitherto professional aspects of our work (although the idea of professionalism may too have been a result of the mystification of experience, and the bureaucratication may be a function of demystification). With a tighter job market, with the supply exceeding the demand, we may expect bureaucratic controls to increase proportionately. (2) The notion of "career" will be replaced by "job," and each will be expendable. Docility and timidity inveigh against the <u>ready acceptance</u> of unionism or professionalism, to protect the academic worker. In the absence of severe union controls, what countermeasures occur will be of the most timid, half-hearted sort. (3) As form replaced content in priority, quantity will replace quality. Increasingly, the number of articles written and the number of papers delivered will be considered more important than the quality of these products. In the teaching area, an eight to five routine may become mandatory, with a panel choosing the textbooks, deciding the amount and type of material to be covered in a course, etc. (4) Lastly, and perhaps most importantly, the aesthetic dimensions of our work (another mystification?) which cannot be measured, and to measure them does them violence, will be replaced by the equivalent of the McGuffy reader. What is not quantifiable for the politicians and cost accountants will not be allowed.

We have built an educational edifice of profound proportions. The coordination of quite complex tasks necessary to administer that edifice is actually staggering. But again, our penchant for form has held sway over our concern for content. In this case, the content of the subject matter need not be examined, but the content of what has been done to us and what we in turn are doing to our students, must be fully explored. We can mystify these relationships and blissfully carry on, but we can expect that we will increasingly pay the price of such mystification. The person we "turn out," as the person we have turned out to be, and the relationship of each to the other, is certainly deserving of more exploration. To do otherwise may reap a whirlwind of which few of us would like to see or from which few of us would be able to profit.

NOTES

*   Text of a paper read at meetings of the
    Community College Social Science Association,
    November 2-4, 1972, and appears in the
    Community College Social Science Quarterly,
    Fall, 1973.

1. Philip Slater, The Pursuit of Loneliness: Ameri-
    can Culture at the Breaking Point, Boston:
    Beacon Press, 1972, p. 59.

2. R. D. Laing, The Politics of Experience, New
    York: Ballantine Books, 1968, pp. 57-76.

3. Ibid., p. 58.

4. Jerry Farber, The Student as Nigger; Essay and
    Stories, North Hollywood, California: Contact
    Books, 1969, p. 122.

Chapter Four

WORK AND POLITICAL CONSERVATISM: A SEXUAL THRUST

H. F. Harlow did a number of experiments where
monkeys were raised not by real mothers but by
surrogate mothers that were wire dummies covered
with terrycloth. During infancy the monkeys formed
strong attachments to these terrycloth surrogates
but when they reached maturity both their capacity
for reproduction and for rearing their own young
was minimal. They were deficient in experience
about mothering, which has often been thought to
be instinctual.[1]

Introduction

One of the main purposes of this chapter is to
try to explain the political conservatism of the
lower, working, and middle classes. Sociologists
have been confronted with some embarrassing phenomena
that we have usually met by ignoring. Marxists, and
many social scientists, have sought to explain arch
conservatism among much of the working class by
utilizing the marxian concept of "false consciousness." This has occurred, despite the injunctions
of the sociology of knowledge and the existential
argument. Rather than seeing man as having choice in
a finitely structured situation, we have been very
quick to promulgate the notions of "false consciousness" and "structural constraint" to explain such
conservatism. These concepts may be seen to very
superficially explain the phenomenon but do more to
"describe" the political orientation and world view
of the working classes. "Structural constraint" may
help explain mere acceptance of rules and injunctions
(as if there is anything mere about acceptance) but
does not seem to do justice to the relatively tenacious embracing of these rules and injunctions. When
such embracing behavior is rationalized (away) by
middle-class sociologists, their theories may be seen
to be due more to their imputation of their own
rationalities and categories of thought upon other
people than to the amount of variance regarding such
embracing behavior that seems to be accounted for by

such notions as "false consciousness" and "structural constraint."

To try to explain "embracing behavior," even under conditions that do not seem rational to middle-class sociologists, we have to go into the biological infrastructure of man and the relationship between his libidinal drives and the routinized power relationships (Weber's notion of "authority"[2]) found in the most pervasive aspect of his life: his work. There may be seen to be an emotional and aesthetic (erotic) cathexis between the individual and his work that should go a long way in accounting for the embracing behavior we are about to describe.

The Derivation of the Proposition

Both Ludwig Feuerbach and the young Marx saw alienation as the destruction of sexuality. "...the alienated man was one who had acquired a horror of his sexual life, and whose whole way of thinking was determined by this repression of sexuality.[3] The alienation of man from himself signified that his natural human emotions had been distorted. 'Alienation signified a mode of life in which man was being compelled by social circumstances to act self destructively,' to cooperate in his own self-mutilation, his castration, that is, the destruction of his own manhood. The economy that men had created presumably to satisfy their needs was finally warping their deepest instincts. Repeatedly the young Marx and Engels characterized the bourgeois society in metaphors and actualities of sexual alienation. Economic exploitation eventuated in the mutilations of sexual alienation."[4]

The derivation of the notion of "alienation" presupposes a philosophical stance very much a part of Western civilization: the inner _versus_ the outer; the internal _versus_ the external; the individual _versus_ the environment; the self _versus_ the other. Indeed, Freud lent further credence to this philosophical stance, most notably in his book _Civilization and Its Discontents._[5] Freud felt that, through the "reality principle," the needs of civilization demanded repression of man's drives. Man's drives (his libido) were seen as inherently antithetical to the requirements of civilization, not only regarding the enhancement of predictability of behavior, but also to enable the harnessing of the sexual drive and redirecting it to do the "necessary work" of society. Superego structures are thus created via the scaffolding of guilt feelings. Internalized controls thus supplement external controls, so that power relations are not only institutionalized, but legitimated through a moral compulsion to obey by the individual. Man's socialization is to this extent biological, and to help explain his responses to rules and injunctions the libidinal underpinings of such conforming and embracing behavior will have to be explored.

In the contemporary theory perhaps Herbert Marcuse comes closest to grappling with this problem. Rather than rely on the historical notion of Freud's "reality principle", which opposes the libidinal needs of the "pleasure principle," Marcuse uses the historically specific notion of "performance principle" which only opposes or need oppose the pleasure principle within a given historical epoch. The basic variable determining and necessitating such opposition and repression is economic. Freud states that society's motive in repressing the instinctual structure is "economic; since it has not means enough to support life for its members without work on their part, it must see to it that the number of these members is restricted and their energies directed away from sexual activities on to their work."[6] Marcuse agrees but sees justification for repression given a scarcity of goods and services to the extent that the perpetuation of the species is threatened. However, when such conditions are absent, such conditions of repression he calls "surplus repression."[7] In other words, he feels that a non-repressive civilization, giving free play to the aesthetic, erotic mode, is possible. He envisions such a society as follows: when society has reached the stage where there is no longer a struggle for existence, and where work has been replaced by play, and the performance principle by contemplation and display (civilized Narcissism) a set of basic transformations follows: "The body in it entirety would become an object of cathexis, a thing to be enjoyed—an instrument of pleasure. This change in the value and scope of libidinal relations would lead to a disintegration of the institutions in which the private interpersonal relations have been organized, particularly the monogamic and patriarchal family."[8] The biological drive becomes a cathected drive. The pleasure principle reveals its own dialectic. The erotic aim of sustaining the entire body as subject-object of pleasure calls for internal refinement of the organism, the intensification of its receptivity, the growth of its sensuousness...."[9]

At least two questions can be levelled at Marcuse's conclusions: (1) Why assume that work--even "alienated labor"--is external to the individual? (2) Why assume that the eroticization of modern man can take place in the absence of work? History may be dialectical, but there may be memory traces that direct and focus libidinal drives. If work is a central life interest for a great period of time, as with the terrycloth mother, it may become one of the few appropriate objects of eroticization. As Lyman and Scott have observed: "Certain groups are spatially deprived of free territiry--that is the ecological conditions that afford opportunities of idiosyncracy and expression of desired identities." There frequently results various kinds of body manipulation, body adornment and body penetration: the modification of inner space.[10] They suggest a hypothesis "that as other forms of free territory are perceived to be foreclosed by certain segments of the society, these segments...will utilize more frequently and intensively the area of body space as a free territory." [11] Work itself may also be seen to be an object of eroticization via such libidinal cathexis. If work is a central life interest for most people,[12] and if it voluntarily or involuntarily pervades most of one's waking hours, and if sexuality is of sufficient importance that it is "the only function of a living organism which extends beyond the individual and secures its connection with its species" then if cognitive dissonance is to be minimized, and if a schizophrenic split between different levels of reality is to be mediated, work must provide some avenue for channeling this sexuality. In fact, Freud suggested such a possibility by saying that work provides an opportinity for a "very considerable discharge of libidinal component impulses, narcissistic, aggressive and erotic."[13] Ives Hendrick was even more direct, in that he felt that work, because it was the gratification of an instinct, yielded pleasure in its efficient performance. In this sense, work pleasure and libidinal pleasure usually coincide since work serves as an outlet for the discharge of surplus libidinal tension.[14]

Indeed, this seems to be the philosophical assumption that Freud used when viewing sexuality

as harnessed and redirected to do the necessary work
of civilization. It is all that preposterous, then,
to see that sexuality, not only implicated in the
work situation, but as a very vital part of that
situation? To the degree that work cannot exist without the harnessing sexuality, it may be seen that it
is to that degree that there is a libidinal cathexis
with the work itself. Such cathexis may be seen to
be part and parcel of the sexualization of commodities and the occupational attitudes toward sex.
Some examples of such phenomena will follow. In
describing the sexualization of commodities, Philip
Slater states: "The act of buying has become so
sexualized in our society that packaging has become a
major industry: we must even wrap a small purchase
before carrying it from the store to our home.
Carrying naked purchases down the street in broad
daylight seems indecent to Americans (Europeans can
still do it but are becoming increasingly uneasy as
advertising in Europe become more sexualized). After
all, if we are induced to buy something because of
the erotic delights that are covertly promised with
it, then buying becomes a sexual act. Indeed, we are
approaching the point where it absorbs more sexual
interest than sex itself. When this happens people
will be more comfortable walking in the street nude
than with an unwrapped purchase. Package modesty
has increased in direct proportion as body modesty
has lessened."[15]

In describing the occupationalization of sex,
Lewis and Brissett show that sex manuals portray sexual activity as work. Indeed, there are seen to be
work schedules, techniques, considerable effort required, et cetera. They suggest that this phenomenon
may be due to our need to justify and dignify play.
They state that this is not disguising man's play as
work: his play has in fact become work.[16]

Such examples point out the eroticization of
commodities, and the occupationalization of sexual
activity. Psychoanalytic theory, moreover, has set
the foundations for the analysis of the eroticization of work, as seen above.

In discussing and analyzing the relationship
between man and his work, the dualities of internal
versus external, man versus environment, etc., may
be inappropriate and merely a function of the rationalities of middle-class intellectuals and laymen,

in mid-twentieth centurn western civilization. Rather
than there being a duality between man and his work,
there may be seen to be an identity between the two,
not merely because of one's acquired concept of self,
economic needs, of social-emotional legitimation in
corporate society, but because of libidinal cathexis.
When sexuality was harnessed for the necessary work
of civilization, a Frankenstein's monster was created,
whereby the work itself became at least as much an
object of sexuality as more traditional objects.

In this connection, the notion of "alienation"
may not only be a result of these middle class rationalities, but only in a most superficial way describe
the relationship between man and his work. Moreover,
the notion of alienation may be generated more from
socially legitimate responses than from the phenom-
enological underpinnings which underlie and are
masked by such rationalities and responses. State-
ments such as the reporting that both alienation from
work and alienation from expressive relations are
found to be more prominent in highly centralized and
highly formalized organizations,[17] and that even
middle-class people increasingly "work at jobs which
are routinized and specialized and over which they
exercise little or no control,"[18] misses the point
of libidinal cathexis. Such notions revolving around
the supposed alienation or estrangement of man from
his work may very well reflect the dualities inherent
in our current view of the world, and not do justice
to alternative explanations of man's relationship to
his work, mediated particularly by the rules and injunctions which most sociologists mistakenly relate
with what I feel to be the inappropriate and, to a
great degree, inaccurate notion of "alienation." As
Marcuse states,[19] technological forces "deliver the
goods" to people, and insofar as their needs (whether
true to false)[20] are not revolutionary, activity
against the relations of production fulfilling those
needs would be not only irrational, but from my point
of view, impossible.

The extent to which man not merely accepts his
work, and the necessity of work itself, but embraces
that work, its felt necessity and the social control
mechanisms of rules and injunctions that are part
and parcel of that work, it is to that extent that
we may see the aftermath of the harnessing of sexuality in work. That aftermath may be seen to be a
libidinal cathexis to that work, to the extent that

erotic gratifications are received by the work itself.
Such gratifications may be seen to be not merely a by-
product of the work, but a justification for engaging
in the work in the first place. To derive such
erotic gratification is a function of socializing influences both on and off the job, perhaps from memory
traces for a time in civilization where the harnessing
of the sexual drive was crucial to the survival of
the species, perhaps from the delights realized from
the fusion of self and work, mind and action. The
conservatism evinced by the working class, the tenacious adherence to the mechanics and way of life
that middle-class intellectuals, through their own
rationalities view as "alienating," can, I believe,
in great part be explained by such a libidinal cathexis with work itself. The dynamics of such a cathexis will now be explored.

The Dynamics of Libidinal Transference

I have tried to show that such notions as
"structural constraints" and "alienation" do not do
justice to the relationship between man and his work,
and may be more a function of the projection of the
frustrations of middle-class intellectuals in mid-
twentieth centurn western civilization than an actual
analysis of that relationship. In the traditional
sociological view, the individual and particularly
the individual as a worker, is treated as the dependent variable, who, through external control and the
forces of socialization, merely accepts the rules and
injunctions embodied in his work, and also merely
accepts the necessity of his working in the first
place. Through our notion of libidinal cathexis, via
the mechanics of libidinal transference (to be discussed below), the voluntaristic dimension of individual choice and action is given much more weight.
The individual is not merely a recipient, he more or
less consciously chooses; the individual does not
merely accept, he more or less consciously embraces.

In a book review I wrote in 1969, I stated the
voluntaristic dimensions of what we are now calling
libidinal cathexis in the following way: "The
student to the teacher; the employee to the employer;
the Army recruit to the officer; no less than the
lover to the beloved may be considered to embrace
willing enslavement for the pleasure that such enslavement provides. Power, prestige, wealth, and
security, no less than love, may serve as the necessary

and sufficient criteria for such enslavement. Such an individual is not necessarily apathetic, as expressed in the popular literature. He is, on the other hand, **very** much involved and committed to his enslavement, since it is mainly through such a sado-masochistic pose that he may reap what are to him the accountrements of success." [21] This pose is not a put-on for purposes of impression management, but is an actual relationship sociologically and phenomenologically dictated by certain libidinal realities. Beyond the contingencies of socialization, memory traces (both ontogenetic and phylogenetic), and the rewards of the fusion of feeling and being, thought and action, lies work as an object of libidinal cathexis and transference due to its physical and psychological salience to the individual, in great part created by civizational needs for the harnessing of sexuality.

The mechanics by which libidinal transference occurs toward work as its object of cathexis, which in turn creates the embracing behavior discussed above, may be enumerated as follows: (1) Man has drives, and these drives comprise Freud's notion of "libido," (2) Man has a finite amount of Libidinal energy. (3) Man has to externalize this energy, for to solely internalize it would do direct biological damage to the organism. (4) Man seeks an object for the direction of his energy. This is the stage of libidinal cathexis. (5) The object he chooses may be historically and spatially specific (as occurred with the terry cloth mother surrogate in Harlow's experiment), and is to a great degree dependent upon its salience to him (involving the amount of time he spends with "it," and its frequency and duration in his consciousness. (6) When there is an excess of definitions favorable to the adoption of the object as an appropriate one for the libidinal cathexis as opposed to another object, such cathexis, even if of a temporary nature, is for the time being complete. [22] (7) When the energy is directed from a culturally approved source and an object grounded in the routine, everyday life of people, toward such an object of salience for the individual, libidinal transference has taken place.

Through such a libidinal transference, traditional objects of eroticism are supplemented by other objects, not so well recognized or sanctioned in the realm of everyday life. But such a lack of sanction in the ideal culture does not deny its phenomeno-

logical existence or its sociological significance.
In contrast to Marcuse, I am suggesting that the
aesthetic mode, which allows the play of orphic and
narcissistic images and norms, coupled with the
rational requisites of civilization, already exists.
These are not dimensions to be sought, as a counter-
force to supposed Promethean culture heroes[23] who
extol the virtues of "toil, productivity and progress,"[24] but are modes of acting and reacting to the
realities of work that not only make that work possible, but make it meaningful and "enjoyable."
Denials, and the logic of everyday life to the con-
trary, the tenacious embracing of Prometheus transforms him into an Orphic-Narcissistic image, in
which one finds not only his work, but himself as
well.

NOTES

1. H. F. Harlow, "The Heterosexual Affectional System in Monkeys," _American Psychologist,_ 17, 1962, pp. 1-9.

2. Talcott Parsons, ed., _The Theory of Social and Economic Organization,_ New York: The Free Press, 1957, p. 328.

3. Lewis S. Feuer, _Marx and the Intellectuals: A Set of Post Ideological Essays,_ New York: Doubleday and Company, Inc., 1969, p. 74.

4. _Ibid.,_ pp. 75-76.

5. Sigmund Freud, _Civilization and Its Discontents,_ London: Hogarth Press, 1949.

6. Sigmund Freud, _A General Introduction to Psychoanalysis,_ New York: Garden City Publishing Company, 1943, p. 273.

7. Herbert Marcuse, _Eros and Civilization: A Philosophical Inquiry into Freud,_ New York: Vintage Books, 1962, p. 32.

8. _Ibid.,_ p. 184.

9. _Ibid.,_ p. 193.

10. Stanford Lyman and Marvin B. Scott, "Territoriality: A Neglected Sociological Dimension," _Social Problems,_ Fall, 1967, Vol 15, pp. 236-249.

11. _Ibid.,_ p. 248.

12. Sigmund Freud, _A General Introduction to Psychoanalysis, op cit.,_ p. 385.

13. Sigmund Freud, _Civilizations and Its Discontents, op cit.,_ p. 34.

14. Herbert Marcuse, _Eros and Civilization, op cit.,_ p. 200.

15. Philip Slater, _The Pursuit of Lonliness: American Culture at the Breaking Point,_ Boston; Beacon

Press, 1970, p. 94.

16. Lionel S. Lewis and Dennis Brissett, "Sex as Work:
     A Study of Avocational Counseling," _Social
     Problems,_ Summer, 1967, Vol. 15, pp. 8-18.

17. Michael Aiken and Jerold Hage, "Organizational
     Alienation: A Comparative Analysis," _American
     Sociological Review_, August, 1966, Vol. 31,
     pp. 497-507.

18. James W. Rinehart, "Affluence and the Embourgeoi-
     sement of the Working Class: A Critical Look,"
     Social Problems, Fall, 1971, Vol. 19, p. 159.

19. Herbert Marcuse, _One Dimensional Man: Studies in
     the Ideology of Advanced Industrial Society,_
     Boston; Beacon Press, 1966.

20. In this connection, who is Marcuse or anyone else
     to label certain needs, whether manipulated or
     imposed upon others or not, as false. He too,
     is a product of his social class and its ration-
     alities--"false" rationalities imposed upon
     others, no more or less false than the needs he
     argues against.

21. Jerry S. Maneker, A Book Review of the _Story of
     O_, by Pauline Reage, (New York: Grove Press,
     1967) _Indian Sociological Bulletin,_ June, 1969.

22. This statement is loosely borrowed from Edwin
     Sutherland's theory of Differential Association.
     See Edwin H. Sutherland and Donald R. Cressey,
     Principles of Criminology, Philadelphia and
     New York: J. B. Lippincott Company, 1966, pp.
     81-82.

23. Herbert Marcuse, _Eros and Civilization, op cit._,
     pp. 144-179.

24. _Ibid.,_ p. 146.

Chapter Five

MADNESS AT WORK*

The Productivity of Madness

If our reach should exceed our grasp, perhaps
contemplation and residence in other than taken-for-
granted realities is a noble endeavor. Such a voluntary or involuntary endeavor might more humanely be
witnessed with awe rather than derision; viewed as
laudable rather than "sick"; treated with respect
rather than "treated." In pragmatic, materialistic
culture, alternative views of aberrant behavior are
not given much credence. Yet our medical view of
insanity or madness fits in quite well with our production-oriented society, with its nuclear family
and awesome religions similarly geared to producing
producers and consuming consumers. The producers we
produce may safely produce ideas; even those ideas
should be production oriented. To produce realms of
unfamiliar images might be tolerated under certain
specific circumstances (for example, among some poets
or artists). However, to live in these realms is
expressly forbidden and, indeed, punished in the name
of therapy and even humanitarianism.

In some so-called primitive societies dwelling
in such unfamiliar houses exalts one to the status
of priest or shaman. In other societies, the warmth
of the extended family or shelter of a begign community can help soothe the sometimes awesome fear of the
dweller. However, in a society such as ours, where
productive (or even unproductive) work is a virtue,
where money creates power and prestige, and where
goods and services can only be bought, the insane are
quite useful. Indeed, it seems we need our insane.
They, too, are a big business--they provide money
for all sorts of people who treat them, who house
them, and who control them. We also need them to
show us who we are, in that they provide us with
visible evidence of our constructions of whom we
are not like. Their role becomes increasinly important as increasing social change and our own personal dislocations resulting from the distress of
painful adaptations cause us to question who we are.
There can't be an "us" without a "them." We've done
this with criminals, with homosexuals, with beatniks,
with hippies, with junkies--why not with the insane?[1]

Our values, ideas, and ideologies are social constructions.[2] These constructions meet the needs we have in adapting to our social institutions. Since we are always adapting and readapting, our constructions are changing to meet these needs and make painful dislocations and adaptations plausible and palatable for us. In this way, our lives have some semblance of meaning and what might have been a shattered sense of self is miraculously restored. The mosaic is partially rebuilt by our insane and other "deviants," and our own fear is the cement that holds the construction together. Indeed, it may therefore be seen that we create what we fear, and fear what we create.

One may neither safely generalize about so-called sane behavior nor about so-called insane behavior, and to attempt to do so would be unproductive. However, one thing that category of behaviors called "insane" have in common is that they have all been officially labelled as such. Moreover, this label is the product of a judgment made by people with certain values and fairly fixed ideas of what constitute normality and abnormality. As R. D. Laing has said, hundreds of millions of "normal" people have in the past fifty years killed hundreds of millions of other normal people.[3] In war, such behavior is laudable. It is therefore not only the given behavior that determines whether the label of "normal" or "abnormal" will be placed, but also how representatives of the dominant value system of our society will react to the given behavior.[4] There seem to be two major criteria that determine such reactions: social class of the subject, and the situation in which the behavior occurs. Money may not buy happiness, but it does buy relative insulation from labels. Here, the eccentricities of the wealthy person become the neuroses or psychoses of the poor. It is no accident that a disproportionate number of lower class people (and undoubtedly, by extension, other people who are also alienated from the decision-making process concerning their own lives) are labelled "psychotic," and populate our state mental hospitals.[5] The situation in which behavior occurs is also crucial to understanding the eventual fate of that person. For example, should I read a paper to you at a professional meeting my behavior would be viewed one way; were I to read that paper at a New Year's Eve party, it would mean something else to you. So, it is not only my behavior that is at issue here, but the situation in which I engage in the behavior. Our label of "insane" or "deviant" is a product of behavior in a given situation and what certain influential people choose to do about it. If there were something inherently "insane" about given behaviors, all of us might be successfully tagged with that label.

Paranoia?

On the door of my office, my secretary taped a poster that reads, "Just because you're paranoid, doesn't mean they're not out to get you." Most people would agree that paranoia is one form of so-called aberrant behavior. In a society that is production oriented and required obedience to its attributions and conformity to its injunctions, paranoia as conventionally defined is not functional and hence not appropriate. The heightened sensitivity of the paranoid if taken seriously might prove embarrassing. For example, let us assume that our subject is deathly afraid of going to work because he feels that he will be killed in the process. His vivid imagination has constructed a scenario that is paralyzing in its totality (much like the scenario we construct of the paranoid). But if we briefly examine this particular example, the paranoia may not seem all that inappropriate. In our society, if a person does not work he or she starves and goes without certain essential goods and services and so do their families, despite food stamps and welfare. If one doesn't work (or have his money work for him), he is at the mercy of a whole host of contingencies and agencies which can either provide or withhold necessary goods and services. When a person imagines such vulnerability attendant upon loss of control over his life and destiny, work takes on a new meaning. Awesome fear of going to work perhaps becomes more understandable.

When this realization is coupled with the ethics of individuality and competition that are so entrenched in our way of life, so that organizational games of one-upmanship and other forms of backstabbing are salient realities in the working world, an awesome fear of going to work becomes even further understandable. Indeed, if we were going to impose labels on people, those who blithely go off to work in the morning and even enjoy work under conditions described above may be seen to have some dysfunction of reason or sensation. It may be these people who are far more dangerous and destructive in their behavior than are most paranoids. It is the former group who can talk of kill ratios, speak unemotionally about war (and about most other things) and who have suspended judgment and affect regarding events that many poets, mystics, artists, scholars and paranoids feel quite keenly and painfully.

My attempt here is not to delve into the nature of paranoia, but to try to demonstrate how our values and institutions of our society determine what types of behaviors we can choose to reward and punish. Moreover, behavior may be seen as a "rational" adaptation to one's environment. One will engage in behavior that has been reinforced either through direct gratification or through some form of recognition. Should there be an absence of such gratification or recognition (either through positive or even negative stroking)[6] the individual might create or discover other worlds more to his or her liking, much as we have created our own.

Our society seems ripe for labels of pathology, for many aspects of our society may be viewed as pathological. The gap between our "ideal culture" (what we say exists) and our "real culture" (what adults learn "really" exists) is so great that guilt puts a blanket on anger. With our Puritan Ethic, guilt is a far more permissable response to the gap than is anger. (Imagine what happens to suppressed rage?) Indeed, guilt's blanket is quite effective for our society in which "adjustment" is such a cherished value. When individuality, competition, and adjustment are extolled as virtues, anger (and some economically non-productive manifestations of guilt) is not only deemed inappropriate but frequently "sick" and "dangerous" as well. The scenario is further mystified by agencies of welfare dedicated to furthering these values in the name of "help" and adjustment. As Sartre has written of Jean Genet, outlaw and playwright: "Of course, he is neither cold nor hungry. He is given board and lodging. But there's the rub—he is _given_ them. This child has had more than enough of gifts. Everything is a gift, including the air he breathes. He has to say 'thank you' for everything. Every minute a gift is put into his hands at the whim of a generosity that leaves its mark on him forever. Every minute Genet moves a little further away from his foster parents. All this bounty _obliges_ him to recognize that they _were not_

obliged to adopt him, to feed him, to take care of him
that they 'owed him nothing,' that he is obliged to
them, that they were quite free not to give him what
he was not free to accept, in short, that he is not
their son. A true son does not have to display his
gratitude. He draws from the family purse, and it is
his father's duty to bring him up. Deprived of everything through the kindness of others, Genet will later
express his hatred of all generosity toward infer-
iors..."[7] In a society such as ours, conventional
sanity is not necessarily a gift and what may be the
gift of insanity is not allowed to be cherished. And
all this in the name of humaneness and treatment. The
aesthetic products of insanity as seen in the works of
such people as William Blake, Vincent van Gogh, Jean
Cocteau, and William Burroughs are frequently over-
looked as being essential components of their crea-
tors' madness; such madness stigmatized and treated
with drugs and confinement; stigmatization and status
degradation.

Madness, The Work Ethic, and Self Actualization

The work ethic, which may be seen to inhibit
self actualization in the form of peak experiences in
the aesthetic modes of life, is not only all-per-
vasive but so powerful as to be mystified whereby
self actualization is felt possible in an oppressive,
ritualized environment. Where rules become ends in
themselves; where there is a premium on thinking in
narrow, rigid categories of thought; where personalities are molded into "methodical, prudent, disciplined"[8] entities; where work is a matter of life
and death in a bureaucratic society, self actualization is seen to be possible. Our socially constructed mystifications become reified and, lo and
behold, work does in fact become a central life
interest and source of self fulfillment for many
people. To the degree that self actualization is
desirable, and that bureaucratic necessities not
only inhibit the attainment of such a goal, but
mystify the experience to allow people to use work
as the vehicle for its attainment, all work organizations share complicity. Some are more deceptive
than others, by allowing "management by objectives"
and "decentralization of decision making," (called
Theory Y in the literature on organizations[9] but
nevertheless have centralized policy making and have
the recourse to suspension or curtailment of one's
livelihood. It is this realization of one's economic

and personal vulnerability that may yield the stigmatized madness of paranoia or the accepted madness of
bureaucratic authoritarianism. The "methodical, prudent, disciplined" who need an inordinate amount of
structure in their lives (and, apparently, in other
people's lives) not only experience this self actualization at work, but are usually powerful and influential enough to expect work to be such a major source
of fulfillment for other people as well. As they have
the power (usually institutional power) to define
sources of fulfillment for others, they thereby also
have the power to define reality and appropriate behavior for other people as well, based upon their own
constructions of this world. When their institutional
power limits the personal autonomy necessary to cultivate the aesthetic mode of one's life, "sanity" not
only becomes a political definition, but a vehicle for
the "treatment" of a politically vulnerable group by
representatives of a politically powerful group. In
this scenario, "mental health" and "madness" are by no
means necessarily contradictory.

Of course, the aesthetic mode of one's life is
not only confined to artistic and poetic images. All
people have the potential for active imaginations and
fantasy lives. It is in the realm of the imagination
that physical and spiritual ecstasy is possible. As
has most frequently been pointed out by Transactional
Analysts, "strokes", or signs of one's recognition,
are essential to life, and in the absence of positive
strokes, negative stroking (such as feeling guilt or
being kicked) is better than no stroking at all.[10]
As we grow older, we might be able to stroke ourselves
with more effectiveness, particularly when most of our
waking hours is spent working and living in relatively
impersonal bureaucratic organizations, where such
positive (or frequently even negative) stroking is
at a premium. Through an active imagination, self
stroking is not only useful but enjoyable; it need
not substitute for stroking by others (although it
frequently has to) but may add a much needed dimension to one's happiness. As we can receive strokes
through an active imagination, we may be seen to
achieve states of self actualization or ecstasy in
the same way. As the social world is constructed out
of our imagination, and as its evils are constructed
out of our imagination, so too are its delights. The
nature of these delights and their intensity are not
only products of our imagination, but need not necessarily be projected into or within other people's

social worlds in order to be enjoyed and cherished (though they must if one is to avoid the label of "insanity"). To the degree that we have institutions in our society that legitimate ecstasy and exist solely or even primarily for that purpose, it is to that degree that an active imagination becomes crucial to prevent an existential withering away of people for whom ecstasy is not a luxury but a necessity of life not obtainable in oppressive institutions. It is a tragic irony that the degree to which an active imagination becomes necessary, it is to that degree that it is suppressed by rigid parenting and other rigid production-oriented institutions. The tragic irony becomes brutal when we realize that it is the functionaries of these oppressive institutions who define unacceptable products of the imagination as symptoms of illness and insist upon the treatment of the "illness" and frequently the "confinement" of the one possessed.

Madness and Ecstasy

Self stroking can provide ecstasy and ecstasy certainly provides strokes. I am not suggesting that madness is always ecstasy. I am suggesting that it can be ecstasy; it can be a rational response to the oppressiveness of ritualized, non-stroking institutions in which both products and people are consumed. It seems ironic and ludicrous that the agents of these institutions are the ones who define needs for ecstasy, define madness, define its treatment, and politically impose their definitions of reality upon others.

If bureaucracy is to survive at the expense of the cultivation of the aesthetic mode, people must be motivated to participate in this enterprise. The fear of deprivation of essential goods and services is the most basic of motivators. To the degree that one keenly realizes that it is in only products of the imagination that ecstasy may be achieved, those for whom ecstasy is a basic necessity or component of life will so cultivate the suitable imagery. Moreover, to the degree that one keenly realizes that he or she is extremely vulnerable to the vagaries of political and economic contingengies in a society, we may expect a greater likelihood of madness. This madness may occur either through conformity to the dictates of the bureaucratic mode or through the labelling by its staunch representatives of others who seek solace from the madness by going mad in a way the representatives neither understand nor condone. This latter type of madness is neither understood nor condoned because it is dysfunctional in a production-oriented society, and, indeed, if left untreated, becomes a revolutionary activity. The staunch representatives of the bureaucratic mode define and treat such madness as a withdrawal or escape. We may see it as a voluntary or an involuntary seeking for truth, as a cultivation of the deepest recesses of the interior life, and as a revolutionary activity. To the degree that it is left untreated and unpunished, it becomes a revolutionary activity that is not only successful in an intellectual sense, but one that can become threatening in a political sense as well.

One of the greatest threats to the bureaucratic mode is the institutionalization of ecstasy. Liberation of consciousness and the reification of images from the unconscious can be ecstatic. If they are painful, ecstasy can emerge through insightful nurturance of the seeker. To "treat" such states as "illness" the society's representatives discount the potential for ecstasy and insight, degrade and stigmatize the one possessed, and are thus enabled to perpetuate the system in which they are so handsomely rewarded. For the mad seeker who does not accept the imposed images of the bureaucrat's madness, the mirror has more or less successfully, even if only temporarily, been turned to the wall.

NOTES

*   Revised version of a paper read at the annual
meetings of the Pacific Sociological Association,
March, 1976.

1.   Kai T. Erikson, <u>Wayward Puritans: A Study in the
Sociology of Deviance</u>, New York: John Wiley and
Sons., Inc., 1966, pp. 3-23.

2.   Alfred Schutz, "Common Sense and Scientific
Interpretation of Human Action," in M. Natanson,
ed., <u>Philosophy of the Social Sciences: A
Reader,</u> New York: Random House, 1963, pp. 302-46.

3.   R. D. Laing, <u>The Politics of Experience,</u> New York:
Ballantine Books, 1968, p. 28.

4.   Howard S. Becker, <u>Outsiders: Studies in the
Sociology of Deviance,</u> New York: The Free Press,
1963, pp. 8-14.

5.   William A. Rushing, "Two Patterns in the Relationship between Social Class and Mental Hospitalization," in W. Rushing, ed., <u>Deviant Behavior and Social Process,</u> Chicago: Rand Mc-
Nally, 1975, pp. 395-402.

6.   Jut Meininger, <u>Success Through Transactional
Analysis,</u> New York: New American Library, 1973,
pp. 25-33.

7.   Jean Paul Sartre, <u>Saint Genet: Actor and Martyr,</u>
New American Library, 1971, p. 9.

8.   Robert Merton, "Bureaucratic Structure and
Personality," In R. Merton, ed., <u>Social Theory
and Social Structure,</u> New York: The Free Press,
1968, pp. 249-260.

9.   See, for example, George Berkeley, <u>The Admini-
strative Revolution: Notes on the Passing of
Organization Man</u>, Englewood Cliffs, N. J.:
Prentice Hall, Inc., 1971.

10.   Jut Meininger, <u>op cit.,</u> p. 32.

Chapter Six

DRUG USE: THE INSTITUTIONALIZATION OF ECSTASY

The discipline of Sociology was founded in a spirit of reform. Teachers and preachers signaled its coming as a way to ameliorate what they perceived to be the ills plaguing their society. Over the past decades, much analysis has been done of many perceived social problems; in recent years that analysis has been increasingly more sophisticated, both quantitatively and qualitatively. Yet, we have forgotten the "promise." We were founded in the spirit of reform but have knowingly and unknowingly wound up as supposedly dispassionate handmaidens of the status quo. It seems that we will increasingly have to become more politically aggressive if we are to be true not only to our promise but true to the spirit of our analyses as well. The so-called drug problem in America is one example of this mandate.

There do not seem to be any institutions in our society where one may achieve ecstasy. Perhaps certain religious experiences yield such peak experiences; for most people, ecstasy-producing or ecstasy-inspiring institutions do not exist. Therefore, various forms of so-called deviant adaptations arise to fill the gap. The better one's socioeconomic status the more we may expect that he/she will experiment with drugs, be they legal or illegal. This correlation has certainly been established for marijuana use.[1] Perhaps this can be explained by relying on Maslow's notion of need hierarchy, where needs for self actualization may be expected to become more salient when one's physiological, safety, affiliative, and esteem needs are met.[2] Therefore, according to this logic, the more prosperous we become, the more we may strive for peak experiences. Whereas both legal and illegal drugs are frequently used to reach these peak states in the best of times, they may also be used to aid in coping with life's problems in times of personal or economic depression. Therefore, whether as an escape mechanism or as an ecstasy-producing mechanism, certain legal and illegal drugs do fill needs of people both in the best and in the worst of times.

I would like to briefly discuss the ecstasy that fills these needs for people. By the nature of my inquiry, my research has been unsystematic. Over the

77

past several years, I have talked with users of a variety of drugs from legally prescribed tranquilizers to illegal marijuana, psychedelics, and opiates. Here, my concern has been with the nature of the "drug ecstasy" and the ecstasy-producing characteristics of various drugs. The drugs that I am concerned with here are Opium, Cocaine, and LSD.

Opium is typically smoked in a pipe, in which the tar-like material is placed. As with marijuana, the smoker holds the smoke deep in his/her lungs and slowly releases it. Opium creates an environment. The effects seem not to be related to the working of one's mind or perceptions as much as to an actual change in the environment of the person. The room, pictures on the walls, other people, seem surrounded by an aura or glow. It is quiet and peaceful. As with narcotics, one may realize he/she has problems, but has better things to do than dwell on them. It is easier to laugh than cry, but neither are worth the effort. Complex solutions are bothersome and unnecessary. The environment is peaceful and by looking at it, you are peaceful.

As opposed to Opium, the ecstasy of Cocaine is seemingly internal. Typically "snorted," it is also diluted and mainlined into the bloodstream via syringe. There is a mystique surrounding the Cocaine high that is further abetted by its great cost (the current typical price being $90 or more a gram). Cocaine gives you confidence and security and a feeling of a quiet strength that leads to peace. The mundane is bothersome, as with narcotics; the mind is open to better enjoy the peace and pleasure of the "now". One doesn't want this feeling to end.

Acid is a psychedelic in that it allows one to see different levels of reality. The possibilities of everyday life are explored in an atmosphere of exhaltation and joy. It is typically a very small tab that is swallowed with liquid. If words do not do justice to the opium or cocaine ecstasy, they actually defame the Acid ecstasy. On Acid, everything pulsates with energy. Colors change and glisten, leaves shine, and the mind projects images via its own film. The realization that all life is energy is coupled with the belief that all life is holy; the specifics of life are unimportant, but life goes on through eternity no matter what one does. Acid is a teacher, as opposed to Cocaine and Opium which produce pleasure (only pleasure). Poetry becomes crystal clear; television images become laughable in their perceived incidiousness. Categories of thought once held to be necessary are no longer so regarded; life situations are brought into a different perspective. As one person told me after his first Acid experience, "I realized how lousy my life was and how I hated my job. I also realized that I brushed by teeth after every meal. Here I was taking such good care of my teeth, all the while I was losing my mind in a job I hated."

Despite the many criticisms of drug use (curiously and politically referred to as "drug abuse"), there are no institutions in our society that provide similar peak experiences or feelings of self actualization for most people in our society. Since frustrated desires for self-actualization experiences can be seen to lead to aggression and violence[3], it is within the purview of social scientists to not only point out this fact, but provide suggested alternatives. At a time when violence has become institutionalized in our society, drug use may be seen to be socially beneficial. Indeed, as long as free space is continually constricted[4] so that there are no perceived frontiers for people to explore in social or ecological space; as long as the bourgeoning middle class has increasing self-actualization needs; as long as the pain of life for many demands respite not only in the absence of pain but in the house of pleasure, drug use may be a viable method of obtaining this needed ecstasy in a simple, quick way.

It is probably incontestable that drugs such as Opium and Cocaine provide what comes closest to being the ultimate high possible; psychedelics, such as Acid, a revered, ever-ready teacher. If our mission as social scientists is to not only analyze institutions and problems of society but to utilize our knowledge to help people, it seems appropriate that we suggest alternative ways of living and knowing based upon that knowledge. This may well be the ultimate thrust of the study of social problems in the future.

For example, if the data support such a contention, and I feel they do, drug-taking pavillions may be set up where people desirious of achieving ecstasy may come together and experience that joy; then subsequently go about their other routines.

Alternative ways of living and knowing should be explored by social and behavioral scientists, their implications openly discussed, and conclusions and contentions posited in a politically aggressive and sophisticated way. Ecstasy is not a luxury but a necessity for many people; the more basic needs of food, clothing, shelter and association are met, the more we may expect increasing numbers of people to seek peak experiences; should be explored by social scientists who should not feel compelled to blindly accept the legal definitions of reality. Social scientists studying "social problems" will increasingly become sensitive to alternative ways to help people become fulfilled as human beings, and present and lobby for those alternatives we as an association can support, and that support will be contingent upon the data of research and discussion, and not upon dictates of the legal definitions of reality.

NOTES

1. Erich Goode, <u>Drugs in American Society,</u> New York: Alfred A. Knopf, Inc., 1972, pp. 36-37.

2. Abraham H. Maslow, <u>Motivation and Personality,</u> New York: Harper and Brothers, 1954, p. 72. The relationship between self actualization and peak experiences is discussed by A. H. Maslow in his paper, "Peak Experiences as Acute Identity Experiences," <u>American Journal of Psychoanalysis,</u> 21, 1961, pp. 254-260.

3. John Dollard, et al., <u>Frustration and Aggression,</u> New Haven: Yale University Press, 1939.

4. Stanford Lyman and Marvin Scott, "Territorality: A Neglected Sociological Dimension," In S. Lyman and M. Scott, <u>A Sociology of the Absurd,</u> New York: Appleton-Century-Crofts, 1970, pp. 89-109.

Chapter Seven

MOTIVATION AND STRUCTURE IN VOLUNTEER WORK*

Introduction

This study was designed to determine the relationships between motivation and work structure
necessary to promoting favorable reactions toward
one's work. People who have dealt with values toward
work held by people in varying occupations[1] or who
have dealt with motivations and its role in eliciting
favorable performance and satisfaction in one's work[2]
have frequently failed to both systematically examine
the relationships between motivation and structural
contingencies, and have similarly failed to study
work groups where financial remuneration is not a
contaminating factor, whose very presence in large
measure prohibits its control. Since in the case of
the volunteer worker significant monetary rewards are
not important, we are presented with a valuable
opportunity for analyzing aspects of work frequently
obscured by economics in conventional occupational
settings.

The most generic issue here involves the criteria
of satisfaction and acceptable performance at work in
the absence of money. Although it is known that "the
desire to work is not to be explained solely in terms
of its instrumental relationship to the attainment of
money but also in terms of its consequences for the
use and development of skills, and the opportunity
to contribute something useful to society,"[3] it is
rare to be able to consider those latter factors, not
only independently of economic considerations, but in
the absence of such considerations. When viewed in
this way, satisfaction with one's work, performance
at work, and tractability to institutional controls
for which performance at work may be seen to be a
plausible indicator, may not only be seen to occur
in the absense of money,[4] but through the consonance
of motivation with one's work situation. It is the
systematic relationship between motivation and work
situation in eliciting favorable reactions to work
that is the major purpose of this chapter.

Methodology

The study took place in a large voluntary

hospital in a borough of New York City. The volunteer department itself has one director, an assistant director, and a secretary, all of whom are paid. The rest of the people who work in the department are volunteers. When the sample was drawn on May 31, 1967, there were 239 volunteers. A sample of 100 persons, using a table of random numbers, was drawn. When substitutions were needed, as when people refused to be interviewed, they were obtained by taking the next person on the list according to the table of random numbers. In sum, twenty-one substitutions were required. Six of the volunteers in the sample refused to be interviewed; two of them moved out of the neighborhood by the time they could be interviewed; two of them were junior volunteers (high school students) and therefore were inappropriate; eight had been incorrectly placed in the card file from which the list of all the "active" volunteers had been obtained and they were no longer active; three "active" volunteers were incapacitated and could not come to the hospital nor could they be interviewed at home. The sample of 100, as well as the population of 239 volunteers, contained both men and women. Since it was belatedly realized that there might be significant differences between male and female volunteers, particularly in regard to their reasons for doing volunteer work, the fourteen males were discarded from the data analysis. This left a sample of 86 volunteers.

One type of volunteer in one particular voluntary hospital in one borough of New York City is being studied. Moreover, this type of volunteer is markedly different from the volunteers frequently described in the literature. The median age of the volunteers in the hospital was 65 years. Seventy-nine percent of our respondents were not doing any paid work; 31 percent belonged to no clubs or groups, nor did they participate in any other activities; 27 percent said they lived alone at the time of the undertaking of volunteer work, and 30 percent said they lived with their spouse; 45 percent of those volunteers who had children said that at the time of undertaking volunteer work, their children were living away from home; 45 percent of our respondents conceived of no other activities that they could do instead of volunteer work at the time they undertook the volunteer work. Clearly, the characteristics of our sample are in striking contrast to the notion of the volunteer as a selfless "ministering angel"[5] or as an active, idealistic, community-oriented woman.[6] Far from using volunteer work as a leisure time activity, away from her family and/or career, our volunteer frequently seeks out volunteer work to replace that work which has been denied her either through contingencies of the aging process, or because of structural contingencies, such as her husband dying, or her children leaving home and starting families of their own. Indeed, many of the women in our sample could be seen as having been forcibly retired, due to these biological and structural contingencies. On the basis of the data, therefore, we cannot generalize the findings and their interpretations to other types of volunteers (such as people who do fund raising.) There is also no basis for treating the hospital in which we did the study as being representative of other hospitals whether they be voluntary or not or in New York City or not.

The Variables

In order to answer the research question, I gathered a variety of data. First of all, I gathered data on "motivation"--the needs, goals or desires of people--for undertaking and continuing in volunteer work. I assumed that there were three major motivations for undertaking and continuing in volunteer work. They are: the desire to help people, by directly or indirectly ministering to their needs-such as giving them water, running errands for them or packing medical kits that will be used to help them; the desire to be with other people, so that one can interact with others and get some feedback from them or else be in the presence of other people to gratify the volunteer's social needs.

The motive "to be with people" denotes a desire to be in the presence of other people, regardless of whether one serves them or not. Here, the desire to help is irrelevant to the desire to be in the company of others. This motive frequently requires for its fulfillment interaction with others and meaningful feedback, where helping can be irrelevant. Of course, one can fill her desire to be with other people by being in contact with patients and serving them. However, I assumed these to be empirically uncommon phenomena. I assumed on the basis of observation and pre-test that many of the respondents regarded patients more as "objects" to be served than as people from whom to get feedback. There are further structural sources for the distinction between these two major motives. Patients are frequently drugged, in some pain or discomfort, and ill. Such characteristics may be seen to both militate against meaningful interaction for the volunteer and perhaps make salient her relative vulnerability to illness ("There but for the grace of God go I"), encouraging her to look elsewhere to fill a need to be with other people. Hence, the need to help may be seen to be distinctly different from the need to be in the company of others for the purpose of socializing, so as to feel useful or at least to take one's mind off her problems. The third major motive was assumed to be the desire to keep busy. Here, the respondent does volunteer work primarily because of the mechanics of the work itself, rather than the humanitarian or social consequences resulting from doing that work. Hence, the emphasis is upon work itself, as distinct from the desire to help people or the desire to be with people.

In addition, data was gathered on the extent to which the "work situation" to which the volunteer was assigned at the hospital served the motives that led her to volunteer in the first place. Types of work situation examined deal with whether the volunteer works with (serves) patients or not (relating to the major motive of the desire to help people); whether the volunteer works with other volunteers or alone (relating to the major motive of the desire to be with other people); whether the work the volunteer does keeps her busy, lets her relax and more or less do what she wants, or falls somewhere between these two poles.

Finally, data was gathered on the volunteer's "reaction to the work." This data deals with continuance in the work, regularity of attendance, commitment, work satisfaction, and job satisfaction among the volunteers. I shall use this third class of data as dependent variables to be associated with the independent and intervening variables represented by the first two classes of data-motivation, and the capacity of the work situation to satisfy the motivations for engaging in volunteer work.

The Variables were measured in the following way:
1. <u>Major Current Motivation</u> for doing the volunteer work was ascertained by sources of satisfaction and dissatisfaction in the work, as explicitly stated by the interviewed

volunteers.** The questionnaire items used are: "What are your reasons for continuing here?" "What do you feel being a volunteer does for you?" These two items were considered together.

2. **Work Situation** was ascertained by asking the director of volunteers the characteristics of each job that volunteers had in the hospital. When the respondent said what job she had, it was coded as to the director's judgment concerning whether the job required: working with patients or not, working with other volunteers or not, the volunteer to keep busy or not.***

3. **Favorable Reactions to volunteer work:**

   A. **Continuance in the Work:** Ascertained by a re-examination of the records of the volunteer department office three years after the interviews to see which of the respondents left volunteer work and which of the respondents remained.

   B. **Regular Attendance:** Ascertained by the volunteer's own statement to the question, "About how many days have you missed work here in the past month?" and validated by the respondent's time card. Where there was a discrepancy, preference was given to the information on her time card. There were seven such discrepancies.

   C. **Commitment:** Ascertained by the volunteer's readiness to leave volunteer work if other opportunities to satisfy her motivations for doing volunteer work would present themselves. The item used to tap this variable was, "How long do you think you will continue as a volunteer in the hospital?" Answers such as, "Until I die" and "As long as I am physically able" were coded as denoting high commitment.

   D. **Work Satisfaction:** Ascertained by

the volunteer's own statement
concerning her satisfaction with
being a volunteer, all aspects
of being a volunteer presumably
considered. The item used was
"Would you say you were very
satisfied to be here, just somewhat satisfied to be here, or
not at all satisfied to be here?"

E.   Job Satisfaction: Ascertained by
the volunteer's own answer to the
question, "Would you say you are
very satisfied to have this particular job you have as a volunteer, just somewhat satisfied, not
too satisfied, or not at all satisfied?" Here, the emphasis is on
the particular job the volunteer has.

The hypothesis to be tested here is as follows:
Favorable reactions will be the greater the more _work
situation_ is in consonance with _current motivations_
for carrying on in volunteer work; and work situations
which are consonant with the current motivations will
be preferred to those which are not.

Findings

The relationships between the volunteer's Stated
Major Current Motivation and her work situation in
eliciting favorable reactions on each of our dependent
variables will now be detailed and explored.

Continuance in the Work and the Inter-
pretation of Tables

The interviews of the volunteers were conducted
in June and July of 1967. In June of 1970, records
in the volunteer office were examined to see who
among the volunteers in the sample had not continued
and who still remained. Forty-six people in the
sample were no longer doing volunteer work in the
hospital. Of those, one had died and seven had left
for reasons of definite illness. Therefore, these
eight people were not used in the analysis of continuance in the work. The Table dealing with continuance in the work tests the hypothesis using as
the dependent variable whether or not respondents
still remained as volunteers three years after the
time they were interviewed.

As was discussed above, working with patients is the work situation that is most consonant with the motivation "to help"; working with other volunteers is most consonant with the motivation "to be with people"; and whether the job keeps one busy or not is most consonant with the desire "to keep busy."

At this juncture, the key as to how to read the tables will be presented and applied to Table 1. However, just as it applies to Table 1, it also applies to the other tables throughout this chapter that show the relationship between work situation and the dependent variables, for each major motivation.

The largest algebraic difference between each pair of rows is expected to occur in the column which represents the motivation that is consonant with the work situation that each pair of rows represents. The Mock Table Illustrates this expectation.

MOCK TABLE

	To Help	To be with People	To keep Busy
With Patients?			
Yes	X		
No			
With Other Volunteers?			
Yes		X	
No			
Job Keeps Volunteer Busy?			
Yes			X
50-50, NO			

The X's for each pair of rows represent the places in the table where I expect the largest algebraic differences to occur. Therefore, I expect the largest algebraic difference between the first pair of rows to occur in the first column, the largest algegraic difference between the second pair of rows to occur in the second column; the largest algebraic difference between the third pair of rows to occur in the third column. It should be noted that the largest algebraic difference means either the largest positive difference between two percentages, or the smallest negative difference between two percentages, for each pair of rows when the set of percentages are compared across the three columns; if some of the percentage differences are positive and others are negative, the largest algebraic difference is the largest positive difference. In addition, the sum of the percentages in each category (for each pair of rows in each column) need not equal 100 percent, since in these three-dimensional tables, only one category of the third dimension (the dependent variable) is reported; to equal 100 percent, its other categories would have to be added.

Moreover, it should be noted that eleven of the respondents either had more than one volunteer job, one of which involved working with patients and the other not working with patients, or else had jobs, in which they sometimes worked with patients, and sometimes did not work with patients. Also, there were nine respondents who either had more than one volunteer job, one of which involved working with other volunteers, and the other not working with other volunteers, or else had jobs where they sometimes worked with other volunteers and sometimes did not work with other volunteers. These "contradictory" cases were not included in the tabulations related to "work situation" in regard to "with patients or not" and "with volunteers or not" respectively. In addition, the motives which could not be discerned were omitted from tabulation.

The numerical base from which each percentage is drawn is placed in parentheses next to the relevant percentage, and is reported in each table. Moreover, the percent on each of the dependent variables for the total sample, for those with each major motivation (regardless of work situation), and for each breakdown of the work situation (regardless of major motivation) are shown in Tables 1 through 5.

I am hypothesizing that there will be a larger algebraic difference in regard to those volunteers who continued in volunteer work when work situation is consonant with the respondent's major current motivation for doing volunteer work than when the work situation is dissonant with or irrelevant to that major current motivation for doing volunteer work.

90

Table 1 only supports this hypothesis in regard
to the motivation "to help." Here the largest algebraic difference between the first pair of rows occurs
in the first column (63 percent, 17 percent). Disconfirmation occurs when the motivation is "to keep busy."
Actually, for the hypothesis to be completely confirmed in this table, the pattern of the largest algebraic differences would have to be the same as in our
mock table. Where there is a deviation from this
pattern, the hypothesis is disconfirmed in that part
of the table where that deviation takes place. Sometimes, as in the base of Table 1, the largest algebraic difference between a pair of rows occurs not
only in the column that would confirm the hypothesis
(in this case, since it was the third pair of rows involved, it would be the third column), but in another
column as well. This occurrence would necessitate
our calling this comparison a "tie."

TABLE 1. Percent Continuing in Volunteer Work From
1967-1970, by Stated Current Motivation and Work
Situation.

Work Situation	Stated Major Current Motivation			All Moti- vations
	To Help	To be with People	To keep Busy	
With Patients?				
Yes	63% (16)	50% (8)	54% (13)	59% (39)
No	17% (6)	50% (10)	46% (13)	38% (29)
With Other Volunteers?				
Yes	75% (4)	64% (14)	38% (8)	54% (24)
No	44% (16)	40% (10)	58% (19)	47% (45)
Job Keeps Volunteer Busy?				
Yes	47% (15)	63% (8)	60% (20)	56% (35)
50-50, No	63% (8)	47% (17)	45% (11)	46% (35)

All Work
Situations   52% (23)   52% (25)   55% (31)

Total Percent Continuing in Volunteer Work: 51% (78)

91

Regular Attendance

Table 2 bears out the hypothesis in regard to absenteeism. In this table, the largest algebraic difference between the first pair of rows, occurs in the first column (47 percent, 38 percent); the largest algebraic difference between the second pair of rows occurs in the second column (67 percent, 33 percent); the largest algebraic difference between the third pair of rows occurs in the third column (36 percent, 45 percent). Therefore, the highest attendance occurs when work situation is in consonance with the major current motivation for continuing in volunteer work as stated by the respondents.

TABLE 2. Percent Without Absense the Month Before Interview, by Stated Major Current Motivation and Work Situation.

Work Situation	Stated Major Current Motivation			All Motivations
	To Help	To be with People	To keep Busy	
With Patients?				
Yes	47% (17)	25% (8)	29% (14)	34$ (41)
No	38% (8)	67% (12)	54% (13)	50% (34)
With Other Volunteers?				
Yes	67% (3)	67% (15)	50% (10)	46% (26)
No	45% (20)	33% (12)	30% (20)	41% (51)
Job Keeps Volunteer Busy?				
Yes	39% (18)	27% (11)	36% (22)	34% (50)
50-50, No	63% (17)	65% (17)	45% (11)	56% (36)

All Work
Situations   46% (26)   50% (28)   39% (33)

Total Percent Without Absenses: 43% (86)

Commitment

Table 3 also shows complete confirmation of the hypothesis. The largest algebraic difference between the first pair of the rows occurs in the first column

(65 percent, 63 percent); the largest algebraic difference between the second pair of rows occurs in the
second column (73 percent, 50 percent); the largest
algebraic difference between the third pair of rows
occurs in the third column (68 percent, 45 percent).

TABLE 3. Percent with High Commitment to Volunteer
Work, by Stated Major Current Motivation and Work
Situation.

| Work Situation | Stated Major Current Motivation | | | All Motivations |
	To Help	To be with People	To keep Busy	
With Patients?				
Yes	65% (17)	38% (8)	50% (14)	54% (41)
No	63% (8)	67% (12)	69% (13)	62% (34)
With Other Volunteers?				
Yes	67% (3)	73% (15)	70% (10)	62% (26)
No	55% (20)	50% (12)	60% (20)	57% (51)
Job Keeps Volunteer Busy?				
Yes	61% (18)	64% (11)	68% (22)	62% (50)
50-50, No	63% (8)	53% (17)	45% (11)	53% (36)

All Work
Situations   65% (26) 57% (28)   61% (33)

Total Percent High Commitment: 58% (86)

Work Satisfaction

Again, the hypothesis is completely confirmed in
regard to work satisfaction. Table 4, the largest
algebraic difference between the first pair of rows,
occurs in the first column (94 percent, 88 percent);
the largest algebraic difference between the second
pair of rows occurs in the second column (100 percent, 67 percent); the largest algebraic difference
between the third pair of rows occurs in the third
column (86 percent, 82 percent).

TABLE 4. Percent Very Satisfied with Work, by Stated Major Current Motivation and Work Situation.

| Work Situation | Stated Major Current Motivation | | | All Motivations |
	To Help	To be with People	To keep Busy	
With Patients?				
Yes	94% (17)	75% (8)	79% (14)	88% (41)
No	88% (8)	75% (12)	85% (13)	76% (34)
With Other Volunteers?				
Yes	67% (20)	100% (15)	80% (10)	85% (26)
No	95% (20)	67% (12)	90% (20)	84% (51)
Job Keeps Volunteer Busy?				
Yes	83% (18)	73% (11)	86% (22)	80% (50)
50-50, No	100% (8)	88% (17)	82% (11)	89% (36)

All Work Situations: 88% (26) 82% (28)   85% (33)

Total Percent Very Satisfied with Work: 84% (86)

Job Satisfaction

In Table 5, the largest algebraic difference between the first pair of rows occurs in the first column (88 percent, 63 percent); the largest algebraic difference between the second pair of rows occurs in the second column (67 percent, 42 percent). Therefore, there is a higher incidence of job satisfaction when there is a consonance of work situation with other volunteer's Stated Major Current Motivation of either helping people or being with people. The hypothesis is not borne out, however, where the major motive is "to keep busy".

TABLE 5. Percent Very Satisfied with Job, by Stated
Major Current Motivation and Work Situation.

| Work Situation | Stated Major Current Motivation | | | All Motivations |
	To Help	To be with People	To keep Busy	
With Patients?				
Yes	88% (17)	63% (8)	64% (14)	76% (41)
No	63% (8)	67% (12)	62% (13)	59% (34)
With Other Volunteers?				
Yes	67% (3)	67% (15)	60% (10)	62% (26)
No	74% (20)	42% (12)	70% (20)	65% (51)
Job Keeps Volunteer Busy?				
Yes	72% (18)	72% (11)	68% (22)	68% (50)
50-50, No	88% (8)	41% (17)	55% (11)	58% (36)

All Work
Situations   77% (26)   57% (28)   64% (33)

Total Percent Very Satisfied with Job: 64% (86)

Work Situation Preferencess

Here, the hypothesis is substantially borne out.
In Table 6, 80 percent of the respondents whose
major motivation is "to help" prefer a job whereby
they work with patients, as compared to only 63 percent of those whose major motive is "to be with
people," and 66 percent of those whose major motive
is "to keep busy." Also, 87 percent of the respondents whose major motive is "to be with people" prefer a job whereby they work with other volunteers,
as compared to only 47 percent of those whose major
motive is "to help" and 75 percent of those whose
major motive is "to keep busy". In regard to the
last pair of rows, there is a tie since 90 percent
of the respondents whose major motive is "to keep
busy" prefer a job that keeps them busy, and 96 percent of the respondents whose major motive is "to
help" prefer a job that keeps them busy.

TABLE 6. **Percent Preferring Work Situations, by**
Stated Major Current Motivation.

| | Stated Major Current Motivation | | |
	To Help	To be with People	To Keep Busy
Prefer: Patients (58)	80%	63%	66%
No Patients (22)	20% (25)	37% (27)	33% (29)
Prefer: Working with other Volunteers (45)	47%	87%	75%
Alone (18)	53% (15)	13% (23)	25% (24)
Prefer: Job Keeps you Busy (68)	96%	73%	90%
Job lets you relax (13)	4% (24)	27% (26)	10% (31)

The following diagram indicates the comparisons
that both confirm and disconfirm the hypothesis, as
well as the ties that are evidenced.

DIAGRAM 1. Tally of Findings with Stated Major
Current Motivation#

	Continuance Table 1	Regular Attendance Table 2	Commitment Table 3
With Patients	C	C	C
With Volunteers	D	C	C
Busy	T	C	C

	Work Satisfaction Table 4	Work Satisfaction Table 5	Work Situation Preferences Table 6
With Patients	C	C	C
With Volunteers	C	C	C
Busy	C	D	T

14 out of 18 comparisons are confirmations (78%)
2 out of 18 comparisons are disconfirmations (11%)
2 out of 18 comparisons are tied (11%)

"C" is "Confirmed"; "D" is "Disconfirmed: "T" is
"Tied"

It can be seen that 14 out of 18 comparisons
confirm the hypothesis. Perhaps the negative findings
in regard to continuance in the work may be due to the
fact that we are relying upon the respondent's account
as to what her motives are doing in volunteer work,
and it may be that many volunteers who did not remain ,
either distorted their responses to the items tapping
mctivation or did not as accurately perceive their
motives as did those volunteers who remained. What
differences that exist between those who left and
those who remained in the volunteer work may in part
be reflected in their accounts as to why they were
doing the work.**** Indeed, it may be that the
accounts of the people who left volunteer work for
reasons other than definite illness are not as trustworthy as those who remained, although the accounts
given by respondents as a whole may not be that

trustworthy either.[7]

One comparison that disconfirmed the hypothesis***** dealt with the major motive of keeping busy and the dependent variable of job satisfaction. Although there are many possible explanations for this disconfirmation, one plausible explanation may be that many people who have as their major motive for doing volunteer work the desire "to keep busy," may have that motive as a vehicle with which to meet such needs as keeping one's mind off herself. Should this be the case, the mechanics of the work may serve to elicit favorable reactions on the other dependent variables, but may not necessarily engender satisfaction with the particular job that acts as such a vehicle. The job here would "merely" be a means to an end, and the other dependent variables may be more likely to reflect this end than the satisfaction with the vehicle that may be bringing these favorable reactions about, especially since the respondent may or may not be aware of this phenomenon. Table 7 shows that more of the respondents who had as their major motive the desire "to keep busy" or "to be with people" had some emotional distress****** within a year or two prior to undertaking volunteer work. As will be seen in the next section, many of the respondents changed their major motives from one to the other of these two motivations. These two motives and their relative interchangeability in this regard, may reflect the use of the job to lessen emotional distress, in that "extrinsic factors" of the job—such as talking with people, seeing people, keeping one's mind off problems, etc.—may be far more rewarding to these people than the mechanics of the work, which may be perceived as necessary only to the extent that the extrinsic rewards are provided.

The only other comparison that did not confirm the hypothesis was the tie that occurred in regard to "work situation preferences" and the motives "to keep busy" and "to help." About the same percentage of people whose major motive was "to help" preferred a job that kept them busy, as the percentage of people whose major motive was in fact "to keep busy." This may be accounted for by the fact that people whose main motivation for doing volunteer work is "to help" feel that the busier they are, the more they can be of help.

In any event, the hypothesis is substantially
borne out, with 78 percent of the comparisons con-
firming the hypothesis. Disregarding that part of
the hypothesis dealing with work situation preferences,
80 percent of the comparisons confirm the hypothesis.

TABLE 7. Stated Major Current Motivation by Emotional
Distress.

	Stated Major Current Motivation		
Emotional Distress	To Help	To be with People	To Keep Busy
Yes	31%	46%	42%
No	69% (26)	54% (28)	58% (33)

Discussion

My concern is not with the existential basis of
motivation as a mode of thought, which has been dealt
with in the Sociology of Knowledge,[8] but with a systematic exploration of the relationship of motivation
with its structural referent, and what relationships
are necessary in yielding favorable performance and
attitudes toward work, where money is not a contaminating factor. The hypothesis was tested using current
motivation rather than original motivation (or the
major motive the respondent had for the first undertaking the volunteer work) since there was found to
be a sizable disjunction between the two. Because
of this disjunction, the hypothesis was not borne out
when the indicator Stated Major Original Motivation
was used. The greatest shift in major motivation
occurred when the major motive was either "to be with
people" or "to keep busy." Whereas 62 percent of the
respondents who said their original motivation for
undertaking the volunteer work was "to help" also
said that was their major current motivation for continuing their work, only 47 percent of the respondents
who said their major original motivation was "to be
with people" and 49 percent of the respondents who

said their major original motivation was "to keep busy" said they had their respective motivations as major current ones.

It may therefore be seen that: (a) many of the respondents changed their motivations since undertaking the volunteer work (which I was not able to account for on the basis of their perception of alternative opportunities available to them to presumably fulfill the motives that prompted them to undertake volunteer work in the first place); (b) those volunteers most likely to change their motives after undertaking the volunteer work may be seen as being the most vulnerable, as reflected in their accounts of their reasons for undertaking the volunteer work. This relative vulnerability of the respondents whose Stated Major Original Motivation for undertaking the volunteer work is "to keep busy" may be plausibly inferred from Table 8. Here 53 percent of the respondents who either had no expectations or did not know what to expect from volunteer work at the time they undertook it,*******said their major reasons for undertaking the volunteer work was "to keep busy," as compared with 25 percent whose major motivation was "to help" and 22 percent whose major motivation was "to be with people".

TABLE 8. Percent of Volunteers Who Did Not Know What To Expect from Volunteer Work, by Stated Major Original Motivation.

	Original Motivation		
	To Help	To Be with People	To keep Busy
Percent Who Did Not know What to Expect	25%	22%	53% (100)

This relative vulnerability of the group whose major motive is "to keep busy" is in part reflective of another inference that can be drawn from Table 8: motivational change may occur because the volunteer at the inception of volunteer work may not have realized the opportunities for other pleasures in volunteer work. We saw that the bulk of motivational change occurred where the major original motivation was "to be with people" and "to keep busy." It would seem that if exposure to volunteer work and the work situation, rather than perceived alternate opportunities, account for motivational change, volunteers

100

with these as major original motivations should not have been as aware of what to expect from volunteer work as would people whose major original motivation is "to help," since they seem to be more stable in that they are not as likely to change their motivation as much. Therefore, we find that volunteers whose major original motivation is "to keep busy" may be conceivably more receptive to elements of the work situation that may satisfy needs that they either did not expect would be satisfied by volunteer work, or they developed needs after undertaking volunteer work that volunteer work may have encouraged, or they found that elements of the volunteer work situation met needs that were hitherto only imperfectly met or even denied through the desire "to keep busy." (The most frequently chosen alternative to keeping busy is the need "to be with people.")

Therefore, the volunteer's work role may effect her personality to the extent that her motivations for engaging in volunteer work may change. Although we saw that respondents whose major original motivation was the desire "to keep busy" were most likely to be receptive to such unanticipated consequences of the volunteer work, this finding does not preclude the possible relationship between role and personality for the other two major original motivations.

Gerth and Mills[9] talk of two types of relationships between "role" and "personality." There is "role-determining personality" whereby the individual is able to let certain personality characteristics help determine one's performance in a given status. Therefore, one adds something to the status; one brings to it certain characteristics perhaps unique to one's self and infuses that status with characteristics hitherto unknown and not necessarily expected. Hence, the role one plays not only differs from that played by those who preceded one but can even color the status whereby other incumbents are similarly expected to play the role in quite the same way.

We believe that many of these volunteers evidence "role-determined personality." Here, the behavioral expectations associated with the status of volunteer (and its sub-statuses, such as members of a group, useful person, and so on) help effect one's personality. By playing a role expected of one in that status, one's concept of self and behavior tendencies may be conditioned on the basis of that role. An example is the "bureaucrat." By playing the role of the bureaucrat, one may become conditioned to subordinate goals to the means one uses to attain them. Being forced by structural constraints to be "methodical, prudent, disciplined,"[10] the bureaucrat changes goals frequently by replacing former goals with the means used to attain them. In short, the means frequently become ends in themselves.

Regarding the volunteers, work situation may engender motivational change. Here, the role can frequently effect the "personality." I have suggested that many of these volunteers would be receptive to this kind of influence of their role.

The desire to "keep busy" may frequently be used as an antidote to boredom or loneliness. It may be used as a refuge from the impulse to dwell upon oneself and one's problems. The desire to have a respite from boredom and/or loneliness may be sufficient to encourage people to undertake volunteer work. Yet, they also come into contact with other people and by such exposure to other people they may develop "friendships" which transforms the desire "to keep busy" from a major need that is not met into one that is either met or is no longer salient to them.

Vulnerable people's relative tractability to contingencies of their work situation may be seen to yield implications regarding their tractability to bureaucratic and other institutional controls even in the absence of money. Not only are favorable reactions to the work elicited when one's Work Situation is consonant with her Major Motivation for doing volunteer work, but the role of current motives is predominant as opposed to the original motives. Tractability to institutional controls may be seen both with regard to favorable performance and attitudes regarding the work as well as to the relative frequency of motivational change so that one's desires are brought into line with the work structure in which she is implicated. With this population, motivation is analytically crucial, both as it determines favorable reactions to the work, and as it seems to reflect the relative vulnerability of this population in the relative frequency of its change, which seems most often to change in the direction of the work situation of the volunteer. In light of these relationships, structure frequently precedes motives, and their interaction (consonance) quite consistently predicts favorable performance and attitudes toward volunteer work.

These volunteers are just one of many different types of volunteers, and they should be treated separately in both theoretical and social policy considerations. The biological, psychological, and social conditions upon which their motivation to do volunteer work is decided, the particular type of volunteer work they either choose or is open to them, given their characteristics and the requirements of the work and their attitudes and performance in the work, as well as the criteria for enhancing favorable attitudes and performance, may be different for these volunteers than for some or all of the other types usually discussed in the literature. The literature not only rarely contains analysis of the elderly volunteer whether inside or outside of the hospital, but does not analyze the criteria of favorable reactions to the work, be the criteria consonance of the work situation with major motivation, or other possible criteria. I feel that this study may not only help fill in this gap in the literature concerning volunteers, but also contribute to analysis of criteria of the favorable reactions to the work among elderly people, where financial considerations become irrelevant and usually do not contaminate such criteria or reactions.

* The study of which this chapter is a partial reflection, was partially supported by a grant from the United States Public Health Service, HS00013. The complete study may be found in "Volunteers, Work and the Worker: A Study of Hospital Volunteers," by Jerry S. Maneker, unpublished Ph.D Dissertation, New York University, June, 1971. I am very grateful for the helpful comments and criticisms of the various drafts of the study provided by Eliot Freidson, Herbert Menzel, and the late Erwin O. Smigel.

** There were other indicators of major current motivation used besides the respondent's account, which yielded different outcomes in the test of this hypothesis.

*** An additional dimension of work situation, "working with members of the staff or not" was tapped and tabulated, but resulted in a disproportionate disconfirmation of the hypothesis, as opposed to the other dimension of work situation consonant with the motive "to be with people," "working with other volunteers or not," which by and large confirmed the hypothesis. Therefore, it was felt that the former dimension was tapping something other than what was being measured, so it was omitted from the analysis.

**** When, in fact, other indicators were used from which to infer the respondent's motivation, the hypothesis was confirmed on this dependent variable. The measures that worked best were relatively open-ended and were: (1) "What do you like about the volunteer job you now have?" (2) "What don't you like about the volunteer job you now have?" (3) "Why would you like this job (that the respondent says she would like best as a volunteer in the hospital)?" (4) "Why wouldn't you like this job (that the respondent says she would dislike most as a volunteer in the hospital)?" (5) "What do you tell people about what you do in the hospital?" These measures were combined to yield an indicator of major current motivation which in regard to continuance in the work completely confirmed the hypothesis.

***** This comparison disconfirmed the hypothesis
regardless of the indicants used to tap Major
Current Motivation.

****** Emotional distress was measured by the
question, "Were you bothered by any worries
or nerves during the year or two before you
began volunteer work?"

******* This information was obtained by the
following item: "In what ways is volunteer
work here different from what you expected
when you took it up?"

1. Elizabeth Lyman, "Occupational Differences in
    the Values Attached to Work," American Journal
    of Sociology, 61, September, 1955, pp. 138-144.
    Herbert Hyman, "The Value Systems of Different
    Classes," in Reinhard Bendix and Seymour Martin
    Lipset, eds., Class, Status and Power: A Reader
    in Social Stratification, Glencoe: The Free
    Press, 1961, pp. 426-442.

2. Frederick Herzberg, et. al., The Motivation
    to Work, New York: John Wiley and Sons, Inc.
    A. Zaleznik, et. al., The Motivation, Produc-
    tivity, and Satisfaction of Workers: A Pre-
    diction Study, Boston: Harvard University
    Press.

3. Victor H. Vroom, Work and Motivation, New York:
    John Wiley and Sons,. Inc., 1964, pp. 43-44.

4. Amitai Etzioni, Modern Organizations, Englewood
    Cliffs, N. J. : Prentice-Hall, Inc., pp. 58-67.

5. Mark Berke, "Why Women Volunteer in the Hospital,"
    In Nathan E. Cohen, ed., The Citizen Volunteer:
    His Responsibility, Role and Opportunity in
    Modern Society, New York: Harper and Brothers,
    1960, pp. 64-69.

6. David L. Sills, The Volunteers: Means and Ends
    in a National Organization, Glencoe: The Free
    Press, 1957.

7. See, for example, Derek Phillips and Kevin J.
    Clancy, "Response Biases in Field Studies of
    Mental Illness," American Sociological Review,
    35, June, 1970, pp. 503-515; Eleanor Maccoby

and Nathan Maccoby, "The Interview: A Total
of Social Science," in Gardner Lindzey, ed.,
Handbook of Social Psychology, Reading,
Massachusetts: Addison-Wesley, Inc., 1954,
p. 482; Irwin Deutscher, "Words and Deeds:
Social Science and Social Policy," Social
Problems, 13, Winter, 1966, pp. 235-254.

8. Karl Mannheim, Ideology and Utopia: An Intro-
duction to the Sociology of Knowledge, New York:
Harcourt, Brace and World, Inc., 1936; Robert
K. Merton, "The Sociology of Knowledge," in
Robert K. Merton, Social Theory and Social
Structure, New York: The Free Press, 1968,
pp. 510-542.

9. Hans Gerth and C. Wright Mills, Character and
Social Structure: The Psychology of Social
Institutions, New York: Harcourt, Brace and
World, 1953, p. 405.

10. Robert K. Merton, "Bureaucratic Structure and
Personality," in Robert K. Merton, op. cit.,
pp. 249-260.

Chapter Eight

A CLASSIFICATION OF GROUPS

Implicit in the literature of sociology is a classification of groups that both orders the groups themselves: a traditional sociological concern; explains a given individual's status relationship to a given group: a contemporary social psychological concern. Although the attempt to so classify groups on an explicit level has been made most notably by Sorokin,[1] his evident biases in classifying groups (for example, as "important" and "not important") detracts from an otherwise notable and noble effort. It will be my attempt to develop a solution to a classical sociological problem that Sorokin and others have grappled with; extend the inquiry to include the social psychological dimension dealing with life space permeation and status-associational relationships. Hence, objective sociological determinants will be the operational indicants necessary for classifying a given group and/or association (here, used synonymously) in a certain way, according to the categories dealt with below. It should be noted, moreover, that an individual's perception of the given group's influence upon him/her or its permeation into his/her life space may be superimposed upon our scheme, thus bridging the two disciplines of sociology and social psychology.

"Institutions," as established ways of fulfilling the desired ends of "groups" so organized for that purpose, as per Mac Iver's distinction between these two terms,[2] may be analyzed similarly on a different level of abstraction. Hence, military, economic, political, religious, kinship, and juridical concerns fall into an ideal-type paradigm, the alternatives of which may be seen to act as ideal-type categories that may be used to so classify these institutions. Relative to Mac Iver's distinction between institution and association (or group), we may note that "the family" may be classified in one way according to our scheme, but "a family" may fall into any one of a number of possibilities or combinations of our categories, with different families differentially classified. Similarly, this distinction holds in that one may belong to an association; he/she can never belong to an institution.[3]

The following is my classificatory system.   A
given group falls into a combination of the following
categories; may be classified as a:

A.   <u>Reference group</u>, in which the person
        is cognitively affiliated with this
        group, whether or not he/she is a
        member of it.   Many examples are pro-
        vided by the phenomenon of anticipa-
        tory socialization where, although
        the individual belongs to one class
        or status-group, he/she affects
        mannerisms, values and standards of
        behavior felt by him/her to be ar-
        ticulated by the status-incumbents
        of the class to which he/she aspires.
        In other words, the individual orients
        himself/herself (or relevant areas of
        his/her life space) within the social
        sphere according to his/her perception
        of the way his/her significant others
        in that class or status-group would
        orient themselves; his/her social
        actions may be expected to be con-
        sonant with that given perception.

A'.   <u>Membership group</u>, in which the individual
        is geographically and/or socially lo-
        cated within a given social structure,
        but does not hold that entity as an
        object to which he/she orients his/
        her aspirations; subordinates what-
        ever rewards and punishments accrue
        to him/her by his/her performance
        within the group from its members to
        those of another group defined above
        as a reference group.   Put social psy-
        chologically his/her ongoing concept
        of self is derived from a social
        structure other than the group under
        study by the sociologist.

A''.   <u>Psycho-Socially Meaningful group</u>, which
        combines the features of both A and A'.
        Here, the individual belongs to the
        group under study and derives his/her
        primary concept of self (with atten-
        dant rewards and punishments gotten for
        his/her performance in that group by
        the members of that group) from that
        group.   This type of group, with this
        particular relationship of the individual

110

to that group, is both a membership group and a reference group.

A'''. Negative Reference group, in which the individual adopts standards and values opposed to those of that group by design.

B. Voluntary group, which contains members who "belong" to it because they desire such membership, whatever their motives may be.

B'. Involuntary group, which contains members who "belong" to it because of psychological or social constraint imposed upon them. The individual may belong to a group purely for instrumental reasons; if such is the case, the group is voluntarily joined because meaningful alternatives to such action were present. If, however, the individual belongs to the group because of psychic or social compulsion, when no other realistic alternatives present themselves, the group is classified as an involuntary group. (Please see below for possible operational indicants.)

B''. Mixed group, which contains both types of people as described in B and B', such as a platoon in the army, where some members enlisted and others were drafted. (Again, arbitrary operational indicants for classification may be set up by the sociologist.)

C. Multibonded group, Sorokin's concepion,[4] in which there is more than one tie uniting the members to each other; hence, to the group itself. The conception of "diffuseness," within the Parsonian framework,[5] in which the individual's life space is permeated in more than one dimension by a given relationship, may be seen to serve as the subjective dimension of the multibonded group as object. A family is a good example of such a group.

C'. Unibonded group, Sorokin's conception[6], in which there is one tie between people in a group to unite them. The subjective dimension on the psycho-social level of analysis corresponds to

Parsons', notion of "specificity,"[7] whereby the given interaction or relationship occurring within the objective dimension of the group effects only one dimension of the individual's life space. Of course, such specific relationships may occur in multibonded groups, just as diffuse relationships may occur in unibonded groups; these occurrences are rare enough to permit the above analysis, especially since such relations will not influence the operational indices which are probably the ultimate criteria of group classification.

D.   System, in which the parts (or statuses) of the group are identifiable, functional to the ongoingness of the group, mutually interdependent, and related to the extent that if one institutes a a change in one part of the "system," another part will be altered as to structure and/or function.

D'.   Congerie, Sorokin's conception,[8] in which there is no necessary patterning of statuses and no necessary functional requisite of their imputed independence. A mob, crowd (for example, spectators at a baseball game) are examples of such groups.

E.   Small group, arbitrarily designated as a group the members of which number less than twenty. A nuclear (or conjugal) family is an example.

E'.   Large group, arbitrarily designated as a group the members of which number more than twenty. An extended family may very well fall into this categroy. Notice here how our separation of these two types of families (the nuclear and the extended) into two discrete categories is consistent with our distinction between institution (here, the family) and association (here, a family).

F.   Primary group, in which there is face to face interaction frequently, but not necessarily, infusing the individual's life space directed toward those affective, emotion-laden accoutrements

of the individual's status both
within the group, and secondarily,
within his/her status in the society
at large.

F'. <u>Secondary group</u>, in which interaction
is externally structured with an eye
toward efficiency; the individual's
achievement in the given structure
holds primacy of orientation, with
affective, emotion-laden accoutrements of the individual's self
serving as a subordinate object of
orientation.

F''. <u>Mixed group</u>, where the group in
question is both a primary group
and a secondary group. A bowling
league is an example of such a
group, where the individual "as a
person" is an object of the orientation of his/her role-set; the individual "as a status-incumbent"
(or achiever) is also an object of
that orientation.

G. <u>Culturally-Bonded group</u>, in which the
group's values adhere to or oppose the
dominant values of the society. An
example is a political party.

G'. <u>Subculturally-Bonded group</u>, in which
the group's values adhere to or oppose
values of a more molecular entity, in
which its members form a subgroup.
The National Association for the
Advancement of Colored People is an
example of such a subgroup which seeks
to press its own interests, addressing
itself to limited values (although they
have wider implications).

H. <u>Democratic group</u>, in which task-
facilitation is pursued, giving all
of the members equal chance to participate both in setting the goals
and in achieving them; in which what
leader there is encourages such give
and take and abides by majority rule.

H'. <u>Authoritarian group</u>, in which task-
facilitation and goal-setting is determined by a leader (elected or
appointed by the group members,
or self-appointed), with no necessary
regard for the wishes of the majority

of the group's members.

H''. <u>Laissez Faire group</u>, in which the leader provides no direction for goal-determination or task-facilitation, and in which the group members themselves have to mediate their differences by determining both norms of action and task and social-emotional policy.

I. <u>Perpetuation-Oriented group</u>, in which the primary orientation is continued existence of the group; where task considerations are developed and articulated with this orientation acting as their determinants.

I'. <u>Task-Oriented group</u>, in which the group is organized for the purpose of solving a problem or attaining a stipulated goal. Its perpetuation is not at issue, here.

I''. <u>Task-Oriented group leading to a Perpetuation-Oriented group,</u> (I'——I), in which a problem-solving group fulfills its task (attains its limited goal) and the members decide, for whatever reason, to perpetuate the group and its norms and values (or create a set of norms and values consonant with the new organization).

I'''. <u>Institutionalized group,</u> in which I and I' are combined. A political party is an example.

Using this combination of a sociological (the "objective dimension") and social psychological (the "subjective dimension") classificatory scheme, I suggest that groups may not only be so classified on their objective dimension as entities, but on the subjective dimension as each relates to a particular individual and his relationship to that group. (Hence, perceptual congruence of the individual with the actual placement of the group by the sociologist, according to his/her arbitrary empirical indicants, may also yield implications for an analysis of marginality and deviance.) Furthermore, the objective dimension may be ascertained operationally by the setting up of indicants by the sociologist: for example, a group may be classified as "primary" if two-thirds or more of its members perceive it as such and/or the sociologist matches the group against his/her criteria for primary group classification, such as they may be. Such indicants may be set up for all of our categories.

As examples of this scheme in operation, we may classify a nuclear family and a political party in the United States on the objective dimension of analysis.

A nuclear family:
$$F_n = (A'') \ (B'') \ (C) \ (D) \ (E) \ (F) \ (G') \ (H) \ (I''').$$

A political party:
$$P_{u.s.} = (A'') \ (B) \ (C') \ (D) \ (E') \ (F') \ (G) \ (H') \ (I'').$$

Of course, some of the categories are questionable; such questions rather than detracting from the scheme may be its strength, for such questioning may lead to further insights into the relative status of the various groups in our society. Furthermore, as indicated above, institutions of our society may be classified ideal-typically according to this scheme: two are classified in the examples above (since these examples deal with ideal type associations which, for present purposes, is operationally synonomous with institution.)

Marginality must be seen as relative to some set of values and/or groups and/or institutions in society. A classification of groups may serve the purposes of both better understanding the nature of the given group and its place in the structure of society, as well as provide a basis of comparison between its more objective and measurable features and the perceptions of its members. The former purpose may be seen to be useful for general sociological theory; the latter purpose may enable us to better understand the nature and degree of marginality of any one person or group of people. For example, using such a classificatory scheme, groups may be categorized according to the features they possess as defined and measured by the sociologist, as has been done with the nuclear family and political party above. Such categorization may also bespeak assumed values and characteristics that in particular cases may not exist. Although most nuclear families may be classified as above, a given nuclear family may not necessarily be so classified. Moreover, by classifying a group in this way, a given individual's perceptions concerning the group and his/her role in it (particularly as they relate to the A, B, and C factors in our classificatory scheme) may more finely specify the nature and degree of his/her marginality to that group, or empirically ascertain if any marginality exists at all.

The classification scheme that I have presented is both tentative and empirically untested. However, I feel that to better understand our subject matter, we must work to develop such a scheme that may not only analytically and empirically clarify various dimensions of groups and their place in society, but also relate the nature of those groups to the perceptions of individuals who are members of those groups. By comparing these perceptions with the measured nature of the given group itself, marginality may be better understood and measured, and the plight of such people as the student, the worker, the mad, the drug user, and the elderly woman tractable to social controls in the absence of financial recompense, may be more fully understood.

NOTES

1. Pitirim A. Sorokin, <u>Society, Culture, and Personality: Their Structure and Dynamics,</u> New York and London: Harper and Brothers Publishers, 1947, pp. 170-178.

2. Robert M. Mac Iver, <u>Society: Its Structure and Changes</u>, New York: Ray Long and Richard R. Smith, Inc., 1948, pp. 12-17.

3. <u>Ibid.,</u> p. 17.

4. Pitirim A. Sorokin, <u>op cit.,</u> p. 171.

5. Talcott Parsons, <u>The Social System</u>, Glencoe: The Free Press, 1951, pp. 65-66.

6. Pitirim A. Sorokin, <u>op cit.,</u> p. 171.

7. Talcott Parsons, <u>op cit.,</u> pp. 65-66.

8. Pitirim A. Sorokin, <u>op cit.,</u> p. 329.

BIOGRAPHICAL STATEMENT

Jerry S. Maneker received his Ph.D in Sociology from New York University in 1971 and was chair of the Sociology Department of California State University, Chico from 1973-1979. His main areas of interest are the study of bureaucracy and of "deviant" behavior, and he is currently doing research on the life styles and careers of psychics. Dr. Maneker is married and has two children. He is also a runner and poet.